A Practical Guide to County Lines, Human Trafficking and Exploitation

Gerwyn Wise
Barrister, Garden Court Chambers

Law Brief Publishing

Published 2024 by Law Brief Publishing, an imprint of Law Brief Publishing Ltd
30 The Parks
Minehead
Somerset
TA24 8BT

www.lawbriefpublishing.com

Paperback: 978-1-916698-58-1

Gerwyn Wise is a criminal defence barrister at Garden Court Chambers. He specialises in cases of organised crime, serious violence, sexual offences, fraud and confiscation.

Gerwyn is frequently instructed to advise and represent individuals involved in high profile county lines and human trafficking operations, particularly those arising out of gang activity. He has expertise representing children and young adults accused of serious criminal offences in both the Crown Court and Youth Court.

Gerwyn has lectured internationally and advised public bodies on the areas of youth justice, modern slavery and child trafficking. He has worked closely with organisations such as the Criminal Bar Association, Bar Council and The Law Society on drafting reforms aimed at ensuring that children and young adults are able to effectively participate in criminal trials.

In his role as Director of Wellbeing and Secretary for the Criminal Bar Association, Gerwyn provided live evidence in front of the House of Commons Justice Committee on the issue of court and tribunal reform.

A Practical Guide to County Lines, Human Trafficking and Exploitation

FOREWORD

I have known and worked with Gerwyn for many years and so it came as no surprise to me that he was writing a book, or that the book he produced was such an interesting and authoritative read. It was also no surprise, having read many of Gerwyn's notes on evidence that he produces for each case he is instructed on, that the book was fundamentally a complete practical guide for practitioners working in this challenging, and constantly evolving, area of law.

Myself and my colleagues constantly represent both youths and adults arrested and charged with cases involving modern slavery and county lines and I have no doubt that my colleagues will find this well referenced book as useful an aid as I will in preparing these cases.

Gerwyn has been instructed on many of our county lines cases and brings a wealth of experience to this subject. His book provides accessible information, and readers can be confident that the text is designed to give immediate assistance to practitioners working under pressure in this complex and challenging area of law. This book, properly understood and widely used, will deepen our understanding of the subject.

This text will guide practitioners through the steps to be taken, and every angle to be considered from the investigation stage to sentencing, when dealing with cases involving county lines and modern slavery, with clarity and practicality. It provides very helpful accounts of recent case law to aid practitioners and makes thoughtful suggestions as to the process to consider at each stage of a case. The book is first rate and is to be thoroughly recommended to practitioners at any stage of their career.

Adrienne Wright
Head of Crime at TV Edwards LLP

PREFACE

"…there is a new form of modern slavery called 'county lines'. I have only recently learned about this, but it is truly shocking and increasing rapidly. Thousands of children are being picked up by gangs and taken to towns and cities a long way away from home. They are locked into rooms; they are carrying and peddling drugs; and, all too often, treated as offenders rather than as victims. They are controlled, abused and exploited."

– Baroness Butler-Sloss, House of Lords debate on 14 December 2017

Over the past decade those of us involved in the criminal justice system have seen the emergence, and subsequent explosion, of prosecutions arising out of 'county lines' operations. It is a subject that has demanded the attention of politicians, law enforcement, reporters and legal professionals. A significant proportion of large, high profile prosecutions that involve organised crime, serious violence, drugs or weapons can be traced back to the county lines activities of urban gangs.

The aim of this book is to provide a practical guide to legal professionals on the topic of county lines, with a particular focus on the criminal law implications for individuals involved in cases of human trafficking and exploitation. The development of the law in this area, particularly since the passing of the Modern Slavery Act in 2015, is both interesting but also necessary knowledge for any practitioner instructed in a county lines case.

Chapter One sets out the definition of 'County Lines' and provides key information about a typical operation.

Chapter Two provides an outline of how the typical 'County Lines' operation works and the various roles undertaken by those involved.

Chapter Three highlights the issue of exploitation, particularly in relation to children and vulnerable adults. The chapter sets out how individuals are exploited and subsequently recruited into drug dealing gangs.

Chapter Four explains how control is exerted over exploited individuals by organisers of county lines operations.

Chapter Five sets out the elements of the criminal offence of human trafficking under s.2 of the Modern Slavery Act 2015. The chapter discusses areas that frequently trouble legal professionals working in this area, such as the meaning of 'arranging or facilitating' travel and 'exploitation' in the Act. The chapter also briefly addresses the associated offence under s.4 of the Act.

Chapter Six sets out the elements of the criminal offence of supplying drugs with particular focus on issues that arise in county lines cases, such as the definition of 'possession' and the potential admissibility of large cash deposits / transfers through an individual's bank accounts.

Chapter Seven sets out the elements of the criminal offence of money laundering contrary to s.329 of the Proceeds of Crime Act 2002.

Chapter Eight addresses the various weapons offences that typically appear in county lines cases, specifically bladed articles, offensive weapons, firearms and ammunition. The chapter highlights Court of Appeal judgments on issues such as the availability of self-defence and the scope of the term 'possession' in relation to firearms.

Chapter Nine sets out the international law underpinning the 'non-punishment' principle and how it is implemented domestically through the CPS four stage test.

Chapter Ten outlines the CPS stage one test for assessing whether an individual is a victim of trafficking or slavery. The National Referral Mechanism process is set out in detail with guidance on the steps that must be taken by legal representatives of potential victims. The chapter also sets out the restrictive approach taken by the Court of Appeal to the admissibility of both decisions of the Single Competent Authority and expert opinion on the issue of human trafficking post-*Brecani.*

Chapter Eleven outlines the CPS stage two test and the availability of the defence of duress in cases of human trafficking. The elements of the defence are set out with detailed analysis on the limited scope of 'threats of death or serious injury' since the Court of Appeal decision in *Vinh van Dao.*

Chapter Twelve outlines the CPS stage three test and the availability of the statutory defence under s.45 of the Modern Slavery Act 2015. The elements of the defence are set out with particular focus on the distinction between adults and children. The Chapter also provides assistance with the interpretation and scope of terms such as 'compelled', 'attributable' and 'relevant characteristics'.

Chapter Thirteen outlines the CPS stage four test and the considerations for all prosecutors when deciding if there is a public interest in proceeding with a prosecution of a credible victim of human trafficking, even in the absence of credible evidence supporting defences of duress or under s.45 of the Modern Slavery Act 2015. The chapter outlines recent developments in the Court of Appeal on the jurisdiction of abuse of process to challenge CPS decisions to prosecute offences that occurred before and after the passing of the Modern Slavery Act 2015.

Chapter Fourteen outlines the sentencing principles in 'County Lines' cases and the tough approach taken by the Court of Appeal.

Chapter Fifteen sets out the relevant law relating to the various ancillary orders that the Court may make in county lines cases, particularly confiscation orders, forfeiture orders, Slavery and Trafficking Prevention Orders, Slavery and Trafficking Risk Orders, Serious Crime Prevention Orders and Sexual Harm Prevention Orders.

The law within this book is up to date to the time of writing on 1 October 2024.

Gerwyn Wise
October 2024

CONTENTS

PART ONE

OVERVIEW OF 'COUNTY LINES'

CHAPTER ONE

WHAT IS 'COUNTY LINES'?

The illegal drugs market in the UK is worth billions of pounds. The increased availability of drugs, particularly class A drugs, has led in recent years to the expansion of drug distribution and supply networks from oversaturated urban areas to smaller, rural areas. This is now recognised and described as so called 'County Lines'

> "'*County Lines' is a term used to describe gangs and organised criminal networks involved in exporting illegal drugs into one or more importing areas (within the UK), using dedicated mobile phone lines or other forms of 'deal line'. They are likely to exploit children and vulnerable adults to move (and store) the drugs and money and they will often use coercion, intimidation, violence (including sexual violence) and weapons.*"
>
> (Home Office, '*Serious Violence Strategy*', April 2018)

The vast majority of county lines operations are run from very large urban areas and cities such as London, Manchester, Liverpool and Birmingham, where the drugs market has expanded to the point of oversaturation i.e. drug supplies and suppliers outnumber the available drug user customer base. The consequence for those drug suppliers has been both a reduction in overall profits as well as an increase in the frequency of violent confrontations with other suppliers seeking to secure the limited customer base.

One solution for drug suppliers has been for them to expand their operations beyond their large urban 'city hub' into smaller cities and rural towns where they have found less competition and opportunities to significantly broaden both their customer base and profits.

CHAPTER TWO

HOW DOES THE 'COUNTY LINES' OPERATION WORK IN PRACTICE?

The typical county lines operation uses the following set up:

- The drug suppliers create a network between the larger 'city hub' and the smaller cities / rural town locations into which drugs, primarily heroin and crack cocaine, are supplied. Although many county lines operations are set up and run by established street gangs or organised crime groups, those of us in the criminal justice system will have experience of smaller, less organised setups run by groups of individuals connected through family, friendship or the local community.

- A mobile telephone number is established in the small city / rural town. It is given a name so that it is clearly identifiable e.g. ABC line. The use of the named drugs line is essential to the success of the business model. It is advertised to local drug users and orders are placed for the supply of drugs through the line. The drugs line is often controlled by an individual, located outside the small city / rural town, who is responsible for directing others, located inside the small city / rural town, to supply the drugs.

- The organisers of the drugs lines frequently exploit children and vulnerable adults to ensure safe storage and supply of the drugs, movement of cash profits back to the 'city hub' and securing accommodation in the small city / rural town. This is often referred to as 'cuckooing'.

- The individuals recruited and exploited by the organisers, in particular young children, frequently travel between the 'city hub' and the small city / rural town to restock the drugs and to deliver cash profits.

- The organisers of the drugs lines use intimidation and violence, including the use of weapons such as knives and firearms, against the exploited individuals.

Due to the explosion of county lines cases in recent years, most legal professionals involved in the criminal justice system will likely have some experience of advising and representing individuals involved in such operations. The emergence of county lines operations, or at least the increased acknowledgement of their existence by those involved in the criminal justice system, has been remarked and ruled upon by the Court of Appeal in several significant cases in recent years. As noted by Lady Justice Hallett in *Karemera and others* [2018] EWCA Crim 1432 (para 1):

> "*To avoid detection and promote the supply of drugs, drug dealers run 'county drug lines' using couriers, often teenagers to take drugs from a large city to towns some distance away. The use of county drug lines is a very worrying development and is a method of supplying drugs that is becoming increasingly prevalent*".

CHAPTER THREE

HOW ARE INDIVIDUALS EXPLOITED IN 'COUNTY LINES' OPERATIONS?

County lines operations are without doubt highly profitable, 24/7 businesses that rely upon the exploitation of others.

Central to the success of any such operation is the ability of the organisers to maintain the drugs line through the efficient and regular recruitment of individuals tasked with undertaking the front-line roles in the small cities / rural towns e.g. cutting and wrapping drugs, runners, debt collectors etc. The individuals targeted for recruitment are almost always either children or vulnerable adults. This is because they are most susceptible to the exploitation techniques used by the organisers of the drugs line.

Legal professionals regularly instructed in county lines cases will know that recruitment of individuals can be done face-to-face, through friendships with pre-existing gang members or, more frequently in recent years, over social media. It is not uncommon for recruiters at the top of the operation to have no physical contact with new recruits as supervision is maintained over social media.

Those tasked with recruitment typically target vulnerable, disenfranchised children; sadly, those tasked with such recruitment will often have been previously targeted themselves in the same way by older members of the gang. Legal professionals working in this area will have had experience advising children recruited because of their special educational needs, mental health issues, disabilities, absent / busy parents or guardians, homelessness or previous convictions; essentially children that the recruiters believe can be easily extracted from pre-existing support networks. The recruitment is often based on a glamourisation of the criminal and gang lifestyle, with pre-existing members presented in videos and photographs on social media in possession of large amounts of cash, designer clothes and jewellery. However, for many of the targeted children, the appeal is often as simple as being welcomed into an established group and enjoying the sense of security instilled by older members of the group.

It is worth noting that the recruiters have shown a willingness to modify their approach to reduce the risk of detection by law enforcement. Legal professionals working in this area will have had recent experience of children under 10 years old and, therefore, the age of criminal responsibility being recruited, as well as so called 'clean skins' i.e. children from settled families already based in the small cities / rural towns.

The recruitment of vulnerable adults often follows the same deliberate process. For example, recruiters are known to approach drug users leaving support meetings and drug rehabilitation facilities with the aim of 'cuckooing' their homes. Cuckooing involves those involved in the drugs line taking over the home of a vulnerable person, often a drug user, and using it as a base for storying and supplying drugs. This is the typical model used by the drugs gangs when setting up base in a new small city / rural town. The vulnerable individual may be targeted under false pretences with no prior knowledge that the drug suppliers were going to use their home to store and supply drugs. The vulnerable individual may have initially offered the use of their home but subsequently regretted their decision; quite often the drug user will have initially permitted access in exchange for a regular supply of drugs but find themselves unable to get the gang to leave their home. The vulnerable individual may have begun an entirely separate sexual relationship with one of the drug suppliers, but that relationship is then used to secure the vulnerable person's compliance with demands to use the home address as a location to store and supply drugs.

Again, it is worth noting that the gang leaders are always prepared to adapt their approach in response to law enforcement agencies. Legal professionals will have had recent experience of drugs lines being set up and run out of legitimate accommodation such as short term lets, guest houses, hotels and even AirBnB bookings. Furthermore, there has been a recent trend to take over small, local businesses such as barber shops, coffee shops and car wash outlets.

CHAPTER FOUR

HOW DO THE ORGANISERS OF THE DRUGS LINE MAINTAIN CONTROL OVER EXPLOITED INDIVIDUALS?

Control of the exploited children and vulnerable adults is exerted in several ways.

It is important that legal professionals involved in this area of work can identify the typical techniques used by gang members to maintain control, particularly given the importance of early identification of potential trafficking and exploitation in the criminal process (see chapter 10 for details).

- **Debt bondage** – individuals are initially either gifted or offered 'buy now, pay later' deals for items such as mobile telephones, food, clothing or drugs. However, when inevitably payment for those items is later demanded and the individual is unable to pay, they are forced by the gang to work off the debt. This debt is almost never considered repaid by the gang.

- **Fabricated debt** – new recruits are robbed of the drugs or cash in their possession in a 'fake robbery' set up by the organisers of the drugs line. The recruit is told that they are now indebted to the gang and must pay back the value of the items lost.

- **Sexual abuse** – new recruits, in particular young girls, engage in sexual relationships with pre-existing gang members. The relationships are used as a tool to exercise control and they are forced to undertake front-line tasks for the drugs gang e.g. bagging, running etc.

- **Threats of and the use of violence** – new recruits are subjected to threats of violence to ensure compliance with directions. Those in control are often in possession of knives and sometimes firearms. The threats, and use, of violence is not restricted to the new recruits and often extends to their family members.

Control is exercised by the drugs gang in many different ways and the above are just a few examples of how exploited individuals are left trapped without an escape. However, legal professionals working in this area will also know that the operators of the drugs gang sometimes take a different approach. Much depends on the particular recruit and the task at hand. For example, it is not uncommon, particularly given the constant professionalisation of the operations, for the county lines set up to be run much like a legitimate business, providing recruits with a regular wage, lunch breaks etc. The ultimate goal is always to ensure the security and success of the drugs line.

PART TWO

CRIMINAL OFFENCES IN 'COUNTY LINES' CASES

CHAPTER FIVE

HUMAN TRAFFICKING

Overview

Sections 2 (human trafficking) and 3 (exploitation) of the Modern Slavery Act 2015 ('MSA 2015') set out the offence of human trafficking. The provisions replaced the previous trafficking offences covered by s.4 of the Asylum and Immigration (Treatment of Claimants etc) Act 2004 ('AAI(TOC)A 2004') and s.59A of the Sexual Offences Act 2003 ('SOA 2003'); the consolidated offence introduced by the MSA 2015 covers trafficking for all forms of exploitation.

Section 2 MSA 2015

The offence of human trafficking is set out at s.2 of the MSA 2015:

> *"(1) A person commits an offence if the person arranges or facilitates the travel of another person ("V") with a view to V being exploited.*
>
> *(2) It is irrelevant whether V consents to the travel (whether V is an adult or a child).*
>
> *(3) A person may in particular arrange or facilitate V's travel by recruiting V, transporting or transferring V, harbouring or receiving V, or transferring or exchanging control over V.*
>
> *(4) A person arranges or facilitates V's travel with a view to V being exploited only if—*

(a) the person intends to exploit V (in any part of the world) during or after the travel, or

(b) the person knows or ought to know that another person is likely to exploit V (in any part of the world) during or after the travel.

(5) "Travel" means—

(a) arriving in, or entering, any country,

(b) departing from any country,

(c) travelling within any country.

(6) A person who is a UK national commits an offence under this section regardless of—

(a) where the arranging or facilitating takes place, or

(b) where the travel takes place.

(7) A person who is not a UK national commits an offence under this section if—

(a) any part of the arranging or facilitating takes place in the United Kingdom, or

(b) the travel consists of arrival in or entry into, departure from, or travel within, the United Kingdom."

Section 2(1) makes it a criminal offence to arrange or facilitate the travel of another person with a view to that person being exploited. Travel is defined in subsection (5) as arriving in, entering, departing or, significantly for the purpose of county lines operations, "*travelling within any country*".

The offence may be committed by a UK national anywhere in the world regardless of where the travel or the arrangement or facilitation of it took place (s.2)(6)). For non-UK nationals, the offence may be committed if any part of the travel or the arrangement or facilitation of it took place in the UK (s.2(7)).

Actus Reus

The meaning of the terms 'arranging' and 'facilitating' travel were addressed by the Court of Appeal in *R v Karemara* [2018] EWCA Crim 1432. The prosecution case was that the defendants controlled and operated drug supply lines between London and Portsmouth, and that teenagers aged between 14 and 16 years old had been used as couriers. On each count the prosecution alleged that the defendants had intentionally arranged or facilitated a courier's travel within the United Kingdom with a view to exploiting the courier in contravention of s.4 of the AAI(TOC)A 2004.

The Court of Appeal was tasked with addressing several issues, particularly the meaning and scope of the terms 'arrange' and 'facilitate'. In her judgment Lady Justice Hallett emphasised the importance of undertaking a "*purposive approach*" when identifying the intent of Parliament when introducing the relevant legislative provisions (para 44). Given the identical statutory purpose and materially similar wording of s.2(1) of the MSA 2015, the subsequent judgment of the Court on the issue provided legal professionals with authoritative guidance when grappling with the interpretation of these terms in human trafficking prosecutions under the MSA 2015. When addressing the meaning of the relevant terms, Lady Justice Hallett stated (para 46):

> "*...the two words 'arranging' and 'facilitating' travel are necessarily broad and should be construed accordingly. 'Arranging' is a common word which in our view needs no further explanation to the jury. 'Arranging' would include such matters as transporting B, procuring a third person to transport B, or buying a ticket for B. 'Facilitating' is*

> *intended to be different from 'arranging' and would include 'making easier'. It is not sensible to lay down precise definitions of these terms."*

The broad definition set out above was subsequently adopted by the High Court in *National Crime Agency v Hussain* [2020] EWHC 432 (Admin) when seeking to find a definition for the term 'facilitate' in s.2(1)(c) of the Serious Crime Act 2007.

In *Karemara* the Court of Appeal considered an argument advanced by the prosecution that a simple instruction such as "*go to Portsmouth*" or "*go by train to [city] and then go to x address*" was capable, in principle, of amounting to 'arranging or facilitating' travel. The argument was unsurprisingly opposed by those representing the appellants. The Court of Appeal did not consider it to be a matter of principle and stated, "*it is possible that in some circumstances a mere direction might suffice, but the question is again one of fact*" (para 47).

In short, there is no fixed list of conduct which may amount to either arranging or facilitating travel, each situation must be separately assessed taking into account the individual circumstances and features present in the evidence.

As set out in s.2(5), the definition of '<u>travel</u>' is very broad and includes travel within the country. Therefore, the movement of exploited individuals between 'city hubs' and small cities / rural towns in county lines operations is clearly covered. For an interesting discussion about the relevance of distance to the issue of travel, legal professionals may want to consider *R v Ali* [2015] EWCA Crim 1279 in the context of trafficking for sexual exploitation. In that case the Court of Appeal stated there was no minimum distance requirement for a journey to count as 'travel' though short distances, such as walking between rooms, may well be excluded. Both the legislation and the caselaw are clear, s.2 is only triggered when there is travel.

The exploited person's <u>consent</u> to the travel, whether as an adult or a child, is irrelevant (s.2(2)). This is a significant provision in the context of county lines prosecutions given many exploited individuals, in particular children, agree to join and work for the drug dealing groups. As stated at paragraph 60 of the judgment in *Karemara,* the provisions were clearly introduced to deal with the "*mischief*" of a vulnerable person having consented and the need to "*protect the young and the vulnerable from their own decision-making.*" Therefore, it follows that the prosecution of individuals under s.2 of the MSA 2015 is not dependent on the availability or willingness of exploited victims giving evidence. Again, this is significant in the context of county lines prosecutions given the children and vulnerable adults targeted and groomed by the organisers of the drugs line very often refuse to co-operate with law enforcement agencies; there will be no bar to a prosecution proceeding and resulting in safe convictions even where the jury never heard directly from any exploited individuals.

Mens Rea

Section 2(4) of the MSA 2015 states that the arrangement or facilitation of travel must be done "*with a view*" to the victim being exploited. Therefore, there is no requirement for the prosecution to present proof of actual exploitation having resulted.

The person charged with arranging or facilitating travel with a view to exploitation would be guilty if they intended to exploit the victim or knew or ought to have known that any other person was likely to exploit the victim. There is no requirement for the prosecution to prove that the person arranging or facilitating the travel was personally responsible for any exploitation or, in respect of the second part of the definition, that the person even intended that the victim would be exploited. As legal professionals working in this area know, the statutory provision is broad in scope and has allowed prosecution agencies to implicate an extensive list of individuals caught up in county lines operations e.g. organisers, line holders, runners, drivers.

There is an interesting debate surrounding the status of individuals who provide or arrange accommodation for the exploited person but had no involvement in the arrangement or facilitation of the travel of the exploited person; as already outlined the requirement for 'travel' under s.2 may mean that such individuals are not caught by the statutory offence (indeed that is clearly envisaged with the inclusion of the word 'may' rather than 'will' in s.2(3) when setting out examples of how an individual arranges or facilitates the victim's travel). As those of us working in this area will know, individuals who harbour victims of exploitation are rarely charged with the substantive offence under s.2. However, the recent experience of this practitioner is that those individuals are increasingly appearing as one of the many named defendants when the gang members are charged with conspiracy to traffic victims of exploitation; this enables the prosecution to prove the case on the basis that each individual, including those providing accommodation and seemingly uninvolved in travel arrangements, shared the common purpose of exploitation.

For the purpose of section 2, the term 'exploitation' is defined exhaustively in section 3 of the MSA 2015. A person is exploited if one or more of the following factors apply:

- The person is the victim of an offence of slavery, servitude and forced or compulsory labour contrary to s.1 MSA 2015 (s.3(2)(a)).
- Something is done to or in respect of the person which involves the sexual offence of taking or permitting to take indecent photographs of children under s.1(1)(a) of the Protection of Children Act 1978 (s.3(3)(a)(i)).
- Something is done to or in respect of the person which involves the sexual offences listed in part 1 of the SOA 2003 i.e. rape, sexual assault, prostitution, child pornography etc (s.3(3)(a)(ii)).

- The person is encouraged, required or expected to do anything which involves the commission of offences relating to organ removal or human tissue sales contrary to s.32 and s.33 of the Human Tissue Act 2004 (s.3(4)(a)).

- The person is subjected to force, threats or deception designed to induce that person to provide a service of any kind, provide another person with benefits of any kind or to enable another person to acquire benefits of any kind (s.3(5)).

- The person is used or there is an attempt to use the person for one of the purposes listed under s.3(5) and that person was chosen for that purpose on the grounds that person is a child, is ill, disabled, or related to a person, in circumstances where a person without the illness, disability or family relationship would likely refuse.

The definition in s.3 is consistent with the combination of trafficking offences previously enforced under both s.4 AAI(TOC)A 2004') and s.59A SOA 2003.

The definition of exploitation in s.3 covers a broad range of circumstances and is sufficiently wide enough to cover individuals exploited as part of county lines operations. In relation to adults, s.3(5) has proven to be particularly broad where county lines organisers have used force, threats or deception. Although the 'service' and 'benefits' typically involve the exploited person undertaking unlawful activities, the provision is not limited to criminal offences and legal professionals will have experience of cases in which exploited individuals have been tasked with lawful activities e.g. purchasing food, vehicles.

Associated offence under s.4 of the MSA 2015

Under section 4 of the MSA 2015, an offence is committed where the person commits any offence with the intention of committing an offence under s.2 of the MSA 2015.

Essentially two separate offences are created because there are different maximum sentences available depending on the qualifying offence committed by the person. If the qualifying offence is either kidnapping or false imprisonment the maximum sentence is life imprisonment (s.5(3)) but only 10 years if any other offence is committed.

This associated offence was introduced to ensure that even those on the periphery of human trafficking who play some part in it are prosecuted and convicted. It demonstrates the determination of those involved in drafting the legislation to take a tough stance on those involved at all levels of county lines operations, although there is a question about its necessity. The provision is very rarely relied upon by the prosecution as more often those on the periphery are charged as part of a conspiracy to traffic under s.2.

CHAPTER SIX

SUPPLY OF DRUGS

The offence for which individuals are most often prosecuted as part of county lines operations is possession of drugs with intent to supply them to another; the alternative offences of being concerned in the supply of drugs or conspiracy to supply drugs are also charged in county lines operations.

The offence of possessing drugs with intent to supply is proven if the prosecution demonstrates the following:

- The substance/product is a controlled drug of class A, B or C.
- The individual was in 'possession' of the controlled drug.
- The individual intended to supply the controlled drug to another.

Controlled drug

A list of controlled drugs of class A, B or C are set out in Schedule 2 of the Misuse of Drugs Act 1971 ('MDA 1971'). Legal professionals will seek to identify evidence that the substance either recovered by law enforcement or referred to in the evidence, such as text messages, was a controlled drug. Often in cases of county lines the task is relatively straightforward as the relevant drugs recovered or referred to in the evidence are diamorphine / heroin (class A), crack cocaine (class A) and sometimes cannabis (class B).

Possession

The meaning of the term 'possession' in the context of drugs supply was addressed by the House of Lords in *Lambert* [2001] UKHL 37. As succinctly put by Lord Hope (para 61):

> "*There are two elements to possession. There is the physical element and there is the mental element. The physical element involves proof that the thing is in the custody of the defendant or subject to his control. The mental element involves proof of knowledge that the thing exists and that it is in his possession*".

The individual must be shown to have custody of or control of something which is, in fact, a controlled drug. Knowledge of the nature of the thing is not necessary. Therefore, a person's ignorance or even a mistake about the type of substance would not prevent that person being in possession provided it turned out to be a controlled drug. Having said that there is a requirement that the person knew that a substance was in their possession i.e. there will be no unlawful possession if someone slipped the substance into the person's pocket without their knowledge.

It is frequently the case in county lines operations that individuals, particularly children and vulnerable adults, are handed packages without being told there are controlled drugs inside. The question that arises for legal professionals is whether, in those circumstances, such individuals will be held to have been in lawful possession of those controlled drugs? The question was addressed by Lord Clyde in *Lambert* (para 126)

> *"In some cases the drug may be found on the accused's person or in his house in a state or situation from which it is immediately obvious that it is a controlled drug. In such cases it may well be that that no question about the accused's knowledge of the nature of the substance may arise. A more difficult problem arises where the drug in question is within some container, such as a box or a bag. But the law here is clear to the effect that if the defendant is in possession of the container and knows that there is something in it, he will be taken to be in possession of the*

> *contents of the container. That was clearly affirmed in McNamara ([1988] 87 Cr App R 246)). Where the drug is in a container, it is sufficient for the prosecution to prove that the defendant had control of the container, that he knew of its existence and that there was something in it, and that the something was in fact the controlled drug which the prosecution alleges it to be. The prosecution does not require to prove that the accused knew that the thing was a controlled drug."*

But what if the child or vulnerable adult tasked with holding the package has no right to open it, to check the contents of whatever was given to them by the more senior gang member?

Some assistance may be provided from the judgment of the same Lord Clyde in the earlier decision of *Warner v Metropolitan Police Commissioner* [1969] 1 A.C. 256 relating to previous drugs legislation and the meaning of the term 'possession'. At page 296 of the judgment Lord Clyde set out his view of the term 'possession', stating:

> *"I think that in criminal matters it is important to have clarity and certainty. I have endeavoured to set out my view as to what the Act denotes by the words "to have in his possession." So far as summary is possible my conclusion is that in a prosecution under section 1, it is for the prosecution to prove (a) that the accused was knowingly in control of some article or thing or substance or package or container in circumstances which had enabled him to know or to discover (or could have enabled him, had he so wished, to know or to discover) what it was that he had before assuming control of it or continuing to be in control of it, and (b) that, whether the accused knew this or not, the article or thing or substance or package or container that he had, consisted of, or contained, a prohibited substance."*

Lord Clyde was supported in his analysis in that judgment by both Lord Pearce, who recognised a category of individuals not "*entitled*" to examine the contents of a package (page 306), and Lord Wilberforce, who stated there would be no possession if a person were given a package but had "*no right to open it*" (page 312). Therefore, legal professionals tasked with representing children or vulnerable adults used as couriers in county lines may have an arguable basis for challenging an assertion of possession. As with many of these issues it will depend on the particular facts of the case. Indeed, Lord Wilberforce added in *Warner* that a package handed over in "*unusual*" circumstances with no explanation may result in an inference that the package was "*accepted with whatever it contained, or that it was handed over so that the holder had the right to possess himself of the contents*" (page 312).

Intention to supply

As outlined above, the prosecution must prove that the individual had the intention of supplying the controlled drugs. The question should be resolved "*by reference to the ordinary natural meaning of the word together with any assistance which may be afforded by the context*" (*Holmes v Chief Constable Merseyside Police* [1976] Crim LR 125).

Legal professionals working in this area need to be particularly mindful about the scope of any prosecution evidence and the use made of it to support or establish an intention to supply. Often in county lines cases there will be evidence of the police recovering large amounts of cash, scales, plastic packaging, cutting agents and large bank transfers into accounts held by those said to be involved in the county lines operation. The starting point for the prosecution will often be to rely upon and put all such matters before the jury; the defence should be prepared to challenge them.

The Court of Appeal in *Morris* [1995] 2 Cr. App. R. 69 provided guidance on how such matters ought to be dealt with by the trial judge. At page 75 of the judgement, Mr Justice Morland stated:

> *"In our judgment evidence of large amounts of money in the possession of a defendant or an extravagant lifestyle on his part, prima facie explicable only if derived from drug dealing, is admissible in cases of*

> *possession of drugs with intent to supply if it is of probative significant to an issue in the case".*

In short, evidence of this type will be admissible only if it provides the jury with assistance on the disputed issues. Therefore, the finding of large sums of cash by police may be admissible, for example, if the explanation were that the defendant didn't like holding money in the bank but nevertheless had large amounts in his bank account. However, it wouldn't likely be admissible to tell the jury of previous cash deposits or transfers outside the relevant indictment period as that would only support an inference of previous drug dealing as opposed to present and active drug dealing (see *Gordon* [1995] 2 Cr. App. R. 61). Therefore, legal professionals will need to carefully review the dates of the indictment, the scope of the prosecution case and the extent of the evidence that is sought to be put before the jury to ensure that it is properly probative of an issue in the case.

CHAPTER SEVEN

MONEY LAUNDERING

County lines setups are frequently large profit-making operations that inevitably produce large amounts of cash. Individuals arrested by police are often caught not only in possession of large amounts of drugs but also large amounts of cash.

Legal professionals will frequently find indictments containing allegations of money laundering, often particularised as possessing, acquiring or using criminal property contrary to s.329 of the Proceeds of Crime Act 2002 ('POCA 2002').

The offence of possessing, acquiring or using criminal property is proven if the prosecution demonstrate the following:

- The individual possessed, acquired or used the property (typically cash in the context of county lines operations);
- The property was sourced, in whole or in part, from criminal activity; and
- The individual knew or suspected that the property was sourced from criminal activity.

The prosecution does not have to prove either dishonesty or knowledge that the property came from criminal behaviour; the prosecution is only required to prove suspicion (s.340(3) POCA 2002).

CHAPTER EIGHT

POSSESSION AND USE OF WEAPONS

Overview

The possession and use of weapons forms a significant part of county lines operations. Those overseeing the operations frequently threaten those lower down the chain, particularly the recruited children and vulnerable adults, with weapons. Even those who are recruited through exploitation are handed weapons to protect themselves while they are in possession of valuable commodity such as drugs or profits. Individuals stopped by police in county lines operations are often found with dangerous weapons such as large machetes, swords, and even firearms.

Having an offensive weapon / article with a blade or point

The most likely offences to follow the discovery of weapons in the context of a county lines operation are either possession of an offensive weapon contrary to s.1(1) of the Prevention of Crime Act 1953 or possession of a bladed article contrary to s.139AA(1) of the Criminal Justice Act 1988.

The law in relation to these offences is very similar.

The offence of having an <u>offensive weapon</u> is proven if the prosecution demonstrates the following:

- The individual had an offensive weapon i.e. "*any article made ('offensive per se') or adapted for use for causing injury to the other person or intended by the person having it with him for such use by him or by some other person*" (s.1(4) of the Prevention of Crime Act 1953);

- The individual was in a public place; and
- The individual had no lawful authority or reasonable excuse to be in possession of the offensive weapon.

Since July 2021 it has been an offence to possess certain offensive weapons in a private place (s.141(1A) of the Criminal Justice Act 1988). A private place is defined as any place other than a public place, school premises, further education premises or a prison (s.141(1C)). For a full list of the weapons covered by s.141(1A) see schedule 1 of the Criminal Justice Act 1988 (Offensive Weapons) Order 1988 (SI 1988 No.2019)

The offence of having an article with a blade or point is proven if the prosecution demonstrates the following:

- The individual had a bladed article;
- The bladed article was not a folding pocketknife or, if it was a folding pocketknife, the cutting edge was longer than 3 inches;
- The individual was in a public place; and
- The individual had no good reason (s.139(4)) or religious reasons, work, national costume (s.139(5)) to be in possession of the bladed article

The question often arises in county lines cases, where children or vulnerable adults are found with weapons given to them by others to protect themselves if attacked while in possession of drugs, whether they are able to rely on self-defence as either a 'reasonable excuse' for an offensive weapon or 'good reason' for a bladed article.

The answer was provided by Lord Widgery LCJ in *Evans v Hughes* (1972) 56 Cr App R 813. At page 817 of the judgment, while dealing with the scope of a reasonable excuse for an offensive weapon, he stated:

> *"...it may be a reasonable excuse for the carrying of an offensive weapon that the carrier is in anticipation of imminent attack and is carrying it for his own personal defence, but what is abundantly clear to my mind is that this Act never intended to sanction the permanent or constant carriage of an offensive weapon merely because of some constant or enduring supposed or actual threat of danger to the carrier"*

The principle set out by Lord Widgery LCJ was subsequently applied in the context of a 'good reason' relating to having an article with a blade or point (*McAuley* [2009] EWCA Crim 2130).

The issue will be a matter for the jury to determine, but much will clearly come down to the imminence of any anticipated attack. In *Evans* a gap of a day or two between a previous attack and the carrying the of weapon was found to be potentially reasonable, while eight days was found to be borderline. Subsequent cases with gaps of 16 days were found to be excessive (see *Bradley v Moss* [1974] Crim LR 430).

Firearms and ammunition

There has been a recent increase in the frequency in which firearms and ammunition have been found during county lines investigations. Legal professionals will no doubt have noticed allegations relating to firearms appearing on indictments alongside those for drugs supply and human trafficking.

The possession and use of firearms and ammunition is overseen by the Firearms Act 1968 ('FA 1968') and the Firearms Act 1997 ('FA 1997'). There are several provisions and, due to the unnecessary complexity of their drafting, they often cause legal professionals some difficulties. The types of offences that typically arise in the context of county lines operations are:

- Possession of a firearm or ammunition without certificates (s.1(1) FA 1968)
- Possession of a prohibited weapon or ammunition (s.5(1) and (1A) FA 1968)
- Possession of a disguised firearm (s.5(1A) FA 1968)
- Possession of a firearm or ammunition with intent to cause fear of violence (s.16A FA 1968)
- Possession of a firearm or ammunition with intent to endanger life or property (s.16 FA 1968)

In the context of county lines, where firearms are often hidden in disclosed locations, given to children to hide in their homes or placed into packages that are not to be opened, the key issue is often one of possession i.e. whether the individual was in possession of the firearm or ammunition. The issue is a simple question of fact and the Court of Appeal has, perhaps understandably, taken a very strict approach to ensure the effectiveness of the prohibitions.

The firearm or ammunition must be either physically in the custody of the person or under their control (*Hassan* [2022] EWCA Crim 786). It is not confined to physical possession. For example, the owner of the firearm will be in possession of the firearm even if it is kept in another person's custody and the owner is not present with it (*Sullivan v Earl of Caithness* [1976]).

The offence is effectively one of strict liability. If the prosecution can prove that the individual knowingly had possession of an article which in fact was a firearm then the offence is committed; ignorance that the article was a firearm is immaterial (*Hussain* (1981) 72 Cr. App. R. 143).

But what of the individual right at the bottom of the chain of command who could not reasonably have known that inside the bag they were tasked to hold was a firearm? Legal professionals involved in this area of work will know that this is frequently the position with children or vulnerable adults in county lines cases.

The answer is clear. An individual would be guilty even if they could not reasonably have been expected to know that the bag contained a firearm, (*Steele* [1993] Crim LR 298). In *Steele* the Court of Appeal approved the direction of the trial judge to the jury that there would be no defence to an individual even if they had custody of a holdall for only a minute and did not know or could not reasonably have been expected to know that it contained a firearm. The justification for taking such a strict approach was set out by the Court of Appeal in *Steele*:

> *"That the legislation thus viewed is draconian in its nature must be accepted. It was no doubt intended to be so. If Parliament had thought it's effect should be mitigated in some way, then the appropriate wording could have been incorporated either originally or, later, by way of amendment. The mischief aimed at is obvious and serious. It is also obvious that it is easy for someone found in possession of a firearm in a holdall or similar container to say that he had been asked to look after it for a short or a longer time by a friend or acquaintance."*

This very broad interpretation of 'possession' in the context of firearms and ammunition has had a significant impact on exploited individuals in county lines cases given the unavailability of the defence under s.45 MSA 2015 (see chapter twelve for details).

PART THREE

REPRESENTING VICTIMS OF COUNTY LINES EXPLOITATION

CHAPTER NINE

THE NON-PUNISHMENT PRINCIPLE

You are instructed to represent an individual that you suspect may be a victim of human trafficking and exploitation in the context of a county lines case. What do you need to know?

The starting point for legal professionals working in this area should be Article 26 of the Council of Europe Convention on Action against Trafficking in Human Beings and Article 8 of the EU Anti-Trafficking Directive 2011/36/EU. In short, those provisions state that national authorities are entitled not to prosecute or impose penalties on victims of trafficking for their involvement in criminal activities which they were compelled to commit.

This is the so called 'non-punishment' principle.

The principle is important for several reasons, particularly in the context of county lines cases. The adoption of the principle into the nation state's criminal justice system inevitably increases the likelihood of genuine victims escaping their trafficking situation and co-operating with law enforcement in the investigation and prosecution of those responsible for their exploitation. The principle acknowledges that victims of trafficking are often given no choice but to engage in criminal activity and, unfortunately, they are too often treated as criminals rather than victims.

Having acknowledged the significance of the 'non-punishment' principle, the Court of Appeal was at pains in *R v LM* [2010] EWCA Crim 2327 to remind legal professionals that it does not provide a complete 'get out of jail' card, stating at para 13:

> *"It is necessary to focus upon what Article 26 does and does not say. It does not say that no trafficked victim should be prosecuted, whatever offence has been committed. It does not say that no trafficked victim should be prosecuted when the offence is in some way connected with or arises out of trafficking. It does not provide a defence which may be advanced before a jury. What it says is no more, but no less, than that careful consideration must be given to whether public policy calls for a prosecution and punishment when the defendant is a trafficked victim and the crime has been committed when he or she was in some manner compelled (in the broad sense) to commit it. Article 26 does not require a blanket immunity from prosecution for trafficked victims."*

In order to give effect to the 'non-punishment' principle and to satisfy the obligations under Article 26, the Crown Prosecution Service has adopted a four stage approach when assessing whether to prosecute potential victims of human trafficking and exploitation. Legal professionals should find the four stage approach a useful guide to follow when representing and advising individuals that may be victims of trafficking and exploitation.

The four stages, giving effect to the non-punishment principle, are:

1. Is there a reason to believe that the individual is a victim of trafficking or slavery?

2. Is there clear evidence of a credible common law defence of duress?

3. Is there clear evidence of a statutory defence under section 45 of the Modern Slavery Act 2015?

4. Is it in the public interest to prosecute?

CHAPTER TEN

IS THERE A REASON TO BELIEVE THAT THE INDIVIDUAL IS A VICTIM OF TRAFFICKING OR SLAVERY?

National Referral Mechanism

The starting point for those concerned about potential victims of human trafficking and exploitation should be the National Referral Mechanism (NRM). It was set up in 2009 to assist victims of trafficking although it was subsequently extended to assist with potential victims of modern slavery on 31 June 2015. The purpose of the NRM is to make it easier for the various agencies involved in a human trafficking and modern slavery case to co-operate and share information about potential victims and improve access to advice, accommodation and support.

Step 1 – Identification of a potential victim of trafficking by the 'first responder'

The first step in the NRM process is for a 'first responder' to make a referral to the Single Competent Authority ('SCA') located within the Home Office, identifying the potential victim of trafficking.

The current statutory and non-statutory first responder organisations are:

- Police forces

- Certain parts of the Home Office:

- UK Visas and Immigration
- Border Force
- Immigration Enforcement
- National Crime Agency
- Local authorities
- Gangmasters and Labour Abuse Authority (GLAA)
- Salvation Army
- Migrant Help
- Medaille Trust
- Kalayaan
- Barnardo's
- Unseen
- NSPCC (CTAC)
- BAWSO
- New Pathways
- Refugee Council

The first responder organisations have several responsibilities, including the following:

- Identify potential victims of modern slavery and recognise the indicators of modern slavery.

- Gather information in order to understand what has happened to them.

- Refer victims into the NRM via the online process. Note: informed consent is required from an adult but not for children under 18 years old.

- Provide a point of contact for the SCA to assist with the Reasonable and Conclusive Grounds decisions (see below) and to request a reconsideration where a first responder believes it is appropriate to do so.

- Advise the law enforcement agency who investigated the original offence and any involved criminal justice agencies, such as the CPS, that trafficking / modern slavery is suspected and there has been a referral.

Under s.52 of the Modern Slavery Act 2015, certain public authorities are required to notify the SCA about all potential victims of trafficking / modern slavery. This statutory requirement covers the police, National Crime Agency and local councils. Therefore, practitioners attending the police station to represent clients arrested as part of county lines operations should be alert to asking the investigating police officers whether they have carefully considered their statutory duty to make a referral to the NRM; this is important as legal representatives do not fall within the criteria of a first responder and will therefore be unable to make a direct referral to the NRM on behalf of their clients, which is a clear gap in the process. If the police, as a first responder, form the view despite your representations that their statutory duty is not activated, you as the legal representative ought to pass on your concerns to one of the other listed first responders.

As already outlined, it is important for legal representatives to identify at the earliest possible stage whether the individual they are advising is the victim of exploitation. Both the Preparation for Effective Trial and Better Case Management forms in the Magistrates' Court and the PTPH form in the Crown Court require the defence representative to confirm whether a defendant is a potential victim of exploitation.

The difficult task for any legal representative is to successfully distinguish between a potential perpetrator and a potential victim of trafficking. This is a complex question given the circle of exploitation, with previous vulnerable recruits being tasked with targeting new vulnerable recruits, that forms the basis for county lines operations. Furthermore, many individuals, in particular young people attracted to the lifestyle, make rational decisions to join and support the drug suppliers and the relationships are not always abusive. The subtle undercurrent of exploitation, coercion, grooming and manipulation can be very difficult to identify.

There are several factors that legal representatives ought to look out for with potential victims of exploitation, which form the basis for a referral to the 'first responder'. Some but not all of the relevant factors were helpfully summarised by the Court of Appeal in *A* [2020] EWCA Crim 1408 (para 53):

- Persistently going missing from school, home, care
- Children travelling to locations or being found in areas they have no obvious connections with, including seaside or market towns
- Unwillingness to explain their whereabouts
- Unexplained acquisition of money, clothes, accessories or mobile phones which they are unable to account for
- Excessive receipt of texts or phone calls

- Children having multiple mobile phone handsets or SIM cards
- Withdrawal or sudden change in personality, behaviour or language used
- Relationships with controlling or older individuals or groups
- Leaving home or care without explanation
- Suspicion of physical assault or unexplained injuries

As outlined in Part 1 of this practical guide, legal professionals must be alert to identifying signs of exploitation from the very start of the criminal proceedings. It will often not be an easy task to identify someone who is the victim of exploitation. The individual may be in a relationship of dependency with other group members. They may fear reprisals for either themselves or family members if caught discussing the group. The individual will likely be mistrustful of authority figures. Significantly they will often be unwilling to accept the label of being a victim.

Step 2 – The SCA's 'reasonable grounds' decision

The SCA is the decision-making body in the United Kingdom when it comes to deciding on a potential victim of human trafficking / modern slavery.

The first part of the decision-making process for the SCA is to assess whether there are "*reasonable grounds*" to believe that the individual is a potential victim of human trafficking. The test for the caseworker is formulated in the form of "*I suspect but cannot prove*" that the individual is a victim.

The Home Office statutory guidance 'Victims of Modern Slavery – Competent Authority guidance' published in April 2019 states that reasonable grounds would not normally be met on the basis of an "*unsubstantiated claim alone without reliable, credible, precise and up to date intelligence or information or evidence of some specific behaviour by the person concerned*". Although there is no burden on the individual to prove that they are a victim, it is not difficult to see how a caseworker could rely upon the guidance to impose requirements upon the individual that run against the spirit of the non-punishment principle, particularly as this first step is often used as an initial filter to weed out claims that are deemed without merit.

The aim of the SCA is to make a reasonable grounds decision within 5 working days of receiving the referral from the first responder.

Following a positive reasonable grounds decision, the individual will be eligible for a period of reflection for 45 days. During that time an adult will be entitled to government funded support; children fall under the statutory responsibility of the local authority.

The primary purpose of the 45 days is to allow the individual time to recover and reflect upon their situation, to escape the influence of the traffickers and to begin the process of making an informed decision on co-operating with the authorities.

Step 3 – The SCA's 'conclusive grounds' decision

The 45-day reflection period is also used by the SCA as an opportunity to obtain further information and evidence as part of the assessment before reaching the 'conclusive grounds' decision. The test for the caseworker is approached on the balance of probabilities, essentially asking the question "*is it more likely than not*" that the individual is a victim of human trafficking.

The time taken to reach the conclusive grounds decision is inevitably affected by the availability of supporting evidence. Legal professionals with experience of the NRM process know that delays are significant and there is a considerable backlog of cases. Although the aim of the SCA is to reach a conclusive grounds decision as soon as possible after the conclusion of the 45-day reflection period, it is common for the SCA to take much longer; even in the current backlogged criminal justice system it is not unusual for a criminal case against a potential victim to have reached trial before the SCA has communicated a conclusive grounds decision.

Following a positive conclusive grounds decision, the individual is formally recognised as a victim of human trafficking. The police and CPS are informed as well as any legal representatives for that individual.

Review and application of the NRM decision

The first responder can request a redetermination of a negative reasonable or conclusive grounds decision with the SCA on behalf of the individual. Any legal challenges to either the reasonable or conclusive grounds decisions are brought by way of judicial review. A negative conclusive grounds decision does not preclude the possibility of mounting a defence under s.45 MSA 2015 (S [2020] EWCA Crim 765).

Prosecutors are required to scrutinise the evidence underpinning any NRM decision, particularly by focusing on how the evidence was analysed, weighed and tested by the SCA. Although the SCA decision is not binding on either the CPS or the Crown Court, unless there was evidence to contradict it or significant evidence that had not been considered, it is likely that the criminal courts would abide by the decision as a finding of fact (see comments of Lord Judge LCJ in *R v L* [2014] 1 All ER 113 at para 28).

All legal professionals are under pressure to identify early on whether an individual might be the victim of exploitation, particularly given the involved process of the NRM referral outlined above and the current delays working through the process. This was noted by the Court of Appeal in *R v D* [2018] EWCA Crim 2995 at paragraphs 21 to 24

> *"21. As a decision has to be taken whether or not to prosecute a VOT [victim of trafficking], it is of importance that wherever possible those who may be VOTs are identified before any plea is taken at court. Indeed in cases where there is a suspicion of trafficking or slavery, the CPS guidance requires prosecutors at the first hearing to request that a plea is not formally entered and to apply for an adjournment for further investigation into the defendant's possible status as the victim of slavery or trafficking.*
>
> *22. The court should be alive to the duties of the prosecution to comply with the guidance where a defendant is a potential credible VOT by reference to the indicators of trafficking published by the UN office on drugs and crime human trafficking and UN global initiative to fight trafficking.*
>
> *23. Should the matter be raised at the first hearing the judge will need to determine, as a matter of judgment on the facts of the individual case, whether a defendant is a potential credible VOT. If he so determines, the case should be adjourned for an NRM referral to be made. This should take 45 days but in practice may be considerably longer.*
>
> *24. In such cases we recognise that the usual stage timetable for case progression under Better Case Management in the Crown Court and Transforming Summary Justice in the Magistrates' Court cannot apply and stage dates will need to be altered to accommodate the referral. Courts will no doubt wish to ensure that VOT questions are not missed. Conversely, we anticipate that courts will be astute to guard against unfounded attempts to raise a VOT point and so cause delay and disruption. Because of the BCM ramifications, we will pass a copy of this judgment to the Senior Presiding Judge for consideration and, if necessary, action."*

Early recognition of the issues is very important. The Court of Appeal has quashed convictions where a guilty plea followed incorrect legal advice that deprived the defendant of a defence. In *R v D*, having noted that the legal representative for the appellant had failed to properly advise his client and follow the NRM process, the Court stated (para 20):

> *"...as has previously been said by this court, the obligation to identify whether a suspect might be a victim of trafficking does not rest on the prosecutor alone. It is incumbent on a suspect's legal representatives in an appropriate case to take steps to ascertain if he had been trafficked and to advise him on the relevant provisions. The court should also be alert to ensure that this has been done. The failure of all parties and the court in this regard led to the potentially inappropriate prosecution and conviction of this applicant."*

The Court of Appeal made similar comments in *R v N* [2019] EWCA Crim 984 where the defence, prosecution and even the judge were criticised for failing to pause proceedings, even at the sentencing stage, to investigate the appellant's claims of human trafficking and exploitation.

And what about the admissibility of any positive NRM decision in criminal proceedings? Legal professionals working in this area will be aware of the recent Court of Appeal judgment in *Brecani* [2021] EWCA Crim 731 where SCA caseworkers were found not to be experts and their decisions little more than inadmissible opinion evidence. As Lord Burnett LCJ stated at para 53:

> *"In this case, and in respect of decisions by case workers assigned to the Competent Authority generally, no information was available upon which it is possible to determine whether and in what area the case worker might be an expert. Beyond an inference that decision making is approached via the comprehensive guidance to which we have referred and that there must be some training provided, case workers in the Competent Authority are junior civil servants performing an administrative function which includes making reasonable grounds and conclusive grounds decisions. The guidance recognises that a decision of the Competent Authority might be disclosed in criminal proceedings but nowhere is there any suggestion that the decision maker might be called to give evidence, still less that in making the decision*

the case worker is acting as an expert and might give evidence in chief and be cross-examined in a criminal court as such."

The reasoning in *Brecani* was affirmed by the Court of Appeal in *AAD* [2022] EWCA Crim 106. The effect of *Brecani* is that a conclusive grounds decision of the SCA and any accompanying minutes will be inadmissible in all circumstances during the trial (although may be admissible in an appeal hearing) as non-expert opinion evidence. The Court in *AAD* confirmed that expert opinion would only be admissible if it is relevant to a matter in issue in the proceedings, the witness is competent to give that opinion and it is needed to prove the Court with information outside the Court's own knowledge and experience (para 85).

Moving forward, the SCA decision about the status of trafficking victims will not be admissible. The door is left open for legal professionals to call expert evidence to address issues of human trafficking and exploitation in county lines cases, although trial judges have already started to deploy a strict, restrictive application of the criteria set out above. The basis for doing so comes straight from the Court of Appeal in Brecani, where the Court warned any such evidence would have to be (para 58):

"...truly expert and not a vehicle to enable the expert to stray into the territory of the jury by expressing his or her personal opinion about whether an account is credible or inconsistencies (are) immaterial...In the right case that evidence might include expert evidence of societal and contextual factors outside the ordinary experience of the jury"

The potential consequence of these recent Court of Appeal decisions is that prosecutors will choose, even where there are clear examples of human trafficking and exploitation, to proceed with prosecutions against the victims. That has certainly been the experience of this legal professional, where the prosecution response to a conclusive grounds decision is often to say to the defence 'well it is a matter for the jury'. Those working in this area may have experienced the situation where all parties, including the prosecution and the Court, agree that the defendant is a victim of trafficking but nevertheless it is right for the prosecution to proceed.

For an interesting example read the Court of Appeal decision in *EK* [2018] EWCA Crim 2961. In that case the appellant had sought to appeal her conviction on the basis that she had previously been trafficked and the decision to prosecute her considering that finding was flawed. The Court of Appeal disagreed, emphasising the seriousness of the offences (controlling prostitution and money laundering) and the appellant's high culpability which would have required a very high level of compulsion to "*extinguish*" the case against her on public interest grounds.

For many working in this area of the criminal justice system, the above approach and direction of the Court of Appeal post-*Brecani* seems to run against the spirit of the non-punishment principle. On one view there appears to be a disconnect between the real-world reality for victims of exploitation and the expectations placed upon them by our criminal justice system; sometimes it is not as simple as walking away or saying no to the oppressor. Furthermore, the adoption of the 'serious offence' qualification in prosecutorial decisions in these cases does not seem to reflect the purpose or wording of the non-punishment principle. Legal professionals will need to keep a close eye on this particular aspect of prosecution decisions moving forward.

CHAPTER ELEVEN

IS THERE CLEAR EVIDENCE OF A CREDIBLE COMMON LAW DEFENCE OF DURESS?

Overview of Duress

The second stage of the CPS four stage test asks whether there is credible evidence of duress and, accordingly, grounds for concluding that there is no realistic prospect of conviction. Legal representatives should be alive to this potential defence and prepared to advise upon it.

An individual who commits a crime under duress may be excused liability. The defence can arise because of threats or from the individual's circumstances. It is for the defence to raise the issue of duress but once raised it is for the prosecution to disprove it.

The defence will not be available to individuals who have voluntarily, by associating with others, exposed themselves to the risk of such duress e.g. by joining a gang (*Sharp* [1987] Q.B 853). In that case the defendant had known the nature of a gang when he voluntarily joined it, knew that he may come under pressure to commit criminal offences and, by the time pressure was exerted upon him, was an active member of the gang. As stated at page 861 of the judgment:

> *"...where a person has voluntarily, and with knowledge of its nature, joined a criminal organisation or gang which he knew might bring pressure on him to commit an offence and was an active member when he was put under such pressure, he cannot avail himself of the defence of duress."*

The strict application of the principle outlined in *Sharp* often creates a significant obstacle for individuals investigated for their role in county lines operations. As outlined elsewhere in this practical guide, the recruitment process is simply not black and white; individuals are frequently targeted because of their particular vulnerabilities, lack of support network and resulting inability to withstand the pressure to join the gang.

Duress by Threats

The elements of the defence of duress by threats were set out in full in *Hasan* [2005] UKHL 22. Lord Bingham, the then senior law lord, started by confirming that it was "*unsurprising that the law in this and other jurisdictions should have been developed so as to confine the defence of duress within narrowly defined limits*" (para 21)

Firstly, the defendant must have reasonably believed that there was a threat of death or serious injury made against them or a member of their immediate family, or someone for whom the person might reasonably feel responsible.

Secondly, the defendant must have reasonably believed that the threats would be carried out almost immediately i.e. that there was no reasonable avenue of escape open to the defendant to avoid the perceived threat.

Thirdly, the threat of death or serious violence was the direct, but not necessarily sole, cause of the defendant committing the offence.

Fourthly, a person of reasonable firmness of the defendant's age, sex and character would have been driven to act as the defendant did. However, the reasonable person need not share the defendant's vulnerability to pressure, timidity or emotional stability arising out of low intelligence as in *Bowen* [1996] 2 Cr. App. R 157 and a drug or alcohol addiction would be excluded as a self-induced condition rather than a characteristic (*Flatt* [1996] Crim LR 576).

Duress by Circumstances

The defence of duress by circumstances, particularly significant in the context of county lines operations, was considered in *Martin* [1989] 88 Cr App R 343. There are two central questions that need to be addressed.

Firstly, was the accused, or may he have been, impelled to act as he did because of what he reasonably believed to be the situation he had good cause to fear that otherwise death or serious physical injury would result?

Secondly, if so, may a sober person of reasonable firmness, sharing the characteristics of the accused, have responded to that situation by acting as the accused acted?

If the answer to both the questions is yes, the accused should be found not guilty.

Limitation to 'threats of death or serious injury'

The requirement for threats and a fear of death or serious injury in the context of the defence of duress has not been considered in any depth by the Court of Appeal since the judgment in *R v Vinh van Dao [2012] EWCA Crim 717* in 2012.

The issue in *Vinh van Dao* was whether threats of false imprisonment were sufficient to leave the defence of duress to the jury. The three Vietnamese appellants in that case had been found by police inside a cannabis factory. They claimed to have been tricked into attending the property. When they attempted to leave, they were threatened and locked inside the property with no means of escape. The appellants' cases were that their roles in the cultivation of the cannabis were done under duress. However, the trial judge refused to direct the jury that the threats of false imprisonment ought to be taken into account when considering the defence of duress. The three appellants were subsequently convicted and applied for leave to appeal. When granting leave, the judge at first instance stated that the case would provide the Court of Appeal with a "*helpful*" opportunity to consider whether a threat of false imprisonment, in the absence of a threat of death or serious injury, would open the door to duress (para 5).

The Court of Appeal dismissed the appeal on the particular facts of the case. However, Lord Justice Gross, in outlining the judgment of the Court, provided a "*provisional view*" on the scope of duress, specifically in relation to the types of threats necessary to establish the defence (para 33). He confirmed that the Court of Appeal would have been "*strongly disinclined*" to accept that a threat of false imprisonment would have sufficed for the purposes of duress. Furthermore, Lord Justice Gross emphasised that although the authorities had not resolved the issue, any such widening of duress would be "*ill-advised*".

The starting point for Lord Justice Gross was the judgement of Lord Simon in *DPP v Lynch* [1975] A.C. 653, where duress was described as (page 686):

> "*...an extremely vague and elusive concept. I take it for present purposes to denote such [well-grounded] fear, produced by threats, of death or grievous bodily harm [or unjustified imprisonment] if a certain act is not done, as overbears the actor's wish not to perform the act, and is effective, at the time of the act, in constraining him to perform it. I am quite uncertain whether the words which I have put in square brackets should be included in any such definition.*"

After highlighting the historical uncertainty in relation to duress, Lord Justice Gross proceeded to emphasise the importance of public policy considerations. Having endorsed the observations of Lord Bingham in *R v Z* [2005] UKHL 22 he went on to note that the defence of duress was "*peculiarly difficult*" for prosecuting authorities to disprove and accordingly ought to be confined within narrow limits (para 38). Lord Justice Gross placed particular significance on the requirement for the prosecution to disprove duress beyond all reasonable doubt when relied on by a defendant (para 45). It was his view that any attempt to expand duress to encompass threats of false imprisonment would allow defendants to make unsubstantiated assertions supported by little evidence; in his words it would create a "*charter for terrorists, gang-leaders and kidnappers*", enabling them to confer criminal immunity on gang members. Therefore, Lord Justice Gross took the view that it would be proper for the Court to "*hesitate*" before expanding the scope and availability of duress (para 46).

Unsurprisingly given those comments the Court of Appeal concluded that the defence of duress should be confined to threats of death or serious injury. In response to submissions that it would be illogical to exclude threats of false imprisonment, Lord Justice Gross argued that it was not illogical and, in any event, the requirements of public policy trumped strict logic (para 49).

The reasoning of the Court of Appeal in *Vinh van Dao* was controversial at the time and it remains so. Lord Justice Gross took the view that the authorities provided limited guidance but, where judicial comment was provided, it pointed towards a narrowing of the defence. It should be noted the authorities referred to in *Vinh van Dao*, including the House of Lords judgment in *R v Z*, did not directly address the question of whether threats of false imprisonment would be enough to establish duress. It was simply not an issue that the judiciary had been previously asked to address.

In his judgment, Lord Justice Gross placed substantial weight upon Lord Simon's judgment in *DPP v Lynch*, stating that it indicated that threats of imprisonment should not lead to a duress defence. It is, therefore, surprising that the comments of Lord Simon were not cited in full by the Court of Appeal, where he went on to state:

> "*...it at least seems to be established that the type of threat which affords a defence must be one of human physical harm (including possibly imprisonment) so that the threat of injury to property is not enough*" (page 606).

It may well be argued, therefore, that Lord Simon specifically envisaged instances where threats of false imprisonment would open the door to duress. Indeed, during the *Vinh van Dao* appeal, counsel for the appellants cited the case of *R v Steane* [1947] K.B. 997 as authority for the submission that threats of imprisonment ought to be within the scope of duress. The defendant in *Steane* had been forced, while imprisoned in a concentration camp, to broadcast messages in Germany during the second world war. He was subsequently charged and convicted of committing an act likely to assist the enemy. The appeal was heard by Lord Goddard, the Lord Chief Justice at that time, who observed "*duress is a matter of defence where a prisoner is forced by fear of violence or imprisonment to do an act which in itself is criminal*" (page 1005). Counsel for the appellants in *Vinh van Dao* submitted that Lord Goddard was clearly of the view that duress encompassed threats of false imprisonment. However, Lord Justice Gross dismissed Lord Goddard's comments as obiter and noted that the defendant in *Steane* was imprisoned in a concentration camp. In his opinion detention in a concentration camp represented a form of imprisonment that could not be "*divorced from the threat of death or serious injury*" (para 35).

A further point raised by the Court of Appeal as justification in *Vinh van Dao* was that the inclusion of threats of false imprisonment, within the scope of duress, would lead to an unacceptable opening of the floodgates. However, as noted by counsel for the appellants during the appeal, there are several alternative judicial constraints on the scope of duress, specifically:

- The threat must be <u>directed</u> against the defendant, his immediate family or someone close to him.

- Duress is only available where the criminal conduct was <u>directly caused</u> by the threat.

- Duress is not available where the defendant could reasonably have been expected to take evasive action e.g. opportunity to involve the police.

- Duress is not available to defendants who voluntarily open themselves up to that duress e.g. voluntarily associating with criminals.

- The tests are stated objectively, requiring the jury to assess the reasonableness of the defendant's perceptions and conduct.

The practical effect of the above pre-existing restrictions is that there already exists a safety net against an inappropriate expansion of or overreliance on the defence of duress. Although raised by counsel for the appellant during the appeal hearing, Lord Justice Gross did not fully address the pre-existing constraints submission. Without further analysis he simply concluded that the Court was "*not persuaded that the other limitations of the defence would furnish a sufficient safeguard against unwarranted over-reliance on the defence*" (para 47). There has been no further judicial comment on this submission since *Vinh van Dao.*

In an apparent attempt to pre-empt accusations that the Court of Appeal had gone too far in restricting the availability of duress, Lord Justice Gross stated that threats of imprisonment could be considered at the sentencing stage. He cited with authority Lord Bingham's judgment in *R v Z*:

> *"If it appears at trial that a defendant acted in response to a degree of coercion but in circumstances where the strict requirements of duress were not satisfied, it is always open to the judge to adjust his sentence to reflect his assessment of the defendant's true culpability" (page 492).*

By way of example, Lord Bingham highlighted the decision of the trial judge in *R v Hudson* [1971] 2 QB 202 to impose a conditional discharge on the defendants where duress was not available. Lord Justice Gross and

Lord Bingham were clearly influenced by a fundamental principle that adults of sound mind should be held responsible for the crimes which they commit. However, the consequence of strictly adhering to such an exacting principle in the context of duress was to severely limit the availability of the defence, particularly for the very vulnerable individuals recruited into county lines operations.

Legal professionals working in this area recognise that the Court of Appeal's judgment in *Vinh van Dao* adds a further, almost insurmountable hurdle for individuals seeking to rely on the common law defence of duress. The practical consequence is to render duress available to only the smallest number of individuals.

But what about those victims of human trafficking and exploitation? In *VSJ* [2017] EWCA Crim 36, the Court of Appeal considered the scope of duress in the context of those victims where the criminal activity occurred before the introduction of the statutory defence under s.45 of the MSA 2015. The submission in that case was that the defence of duress ought to be broadened to cover compelled individuals. The Court of Appeal declined to extend duress to cover victims of human trafficking who were compelled by others to commit crimes. When dismissing the point, Lord Thomas LCJ stated (para 28):

> *"The present law of duress is clear. Its scope and limits are set out in cases of the highest authority. Parliament has considered the position. It enacted s.45 without providing for retrospective protection. In the circumstances it would require instances of clear injustice to justify a court amending the law of duress as applicable to victims of trafficking who were not able to take advantage of the 2015 Act. We have seen no evidence of such instances. The individual cases that were the subject of the decisions in 2010 to 2013 and the appeals and applications being heard by us show that the law operates in practice in a way entirely consistent with the UK's international obligations. We accept that the cases that the court has to consider are cases where the issue as to trafficking often has arisen after the conviction. Changing the law*

> *of duress would not alter that type of case. A court cannot grapple with the issue until it is raised; in some of the cases we are considering it was not raised until after conviction. What has changed is a greater understanding of the position of victims and the need in such cases to investigate. We see no reason to develop the law of duress in the way suggested.*"

Lord Thomas went on to endorse the approach taken by the Court of Appeal in Vinh van Dao, agreeing that "*it would not be right*" to expand the defence even to cover credible victims of trafficking (para 29). Accordingly, it will rarely be possible for individuals implicated in the running of county lines operations to advance a credible defence of duress in the Crown Court.

CHAPTER TWELVE

IS THERE CLEAR EVIDENCE OF A STATUTORY DEFENCE UNDER SECTION 45 OF THE MODERN SLAVERY ACT 2015?

Overview of s.45 statutory defence

The third stage of the CPS four stage test requires consideration of the statutory defence found in s.45 of the MSA 2015. The scope and application of this provision is essential knowledge for any legal representative instructed in a county lines case.

Section 45 creates a specific defence for individuals who may have been the subject of slavery or human trafficking. It does not apply to offences committed before 31 July 2015.

Schedule 4 of the MSA 2015 lists a significant number of offences that are excluded from the ambit of the defence. This includes the most serious offences such as murder, manslaughter, kidnapping, false imprisonment, s.18 wounding/GBH with intent etc. More significantly for county lines cases, allegations of human trafficking and the possession of firearms are also excluded from protection under s.45. It was not intended to cover the whole field of criminal behaviour.

The apparent logic for excluding hundreds of offences, primarily but not exclusively the most serious sexual and violent offences, was to avoid the creation of a legal loophole. Legislators were worried that those charged with the most serious offences would seek to exploit the statutory defence to avoid prosecution. The consequence of that approach is that the gravity of the alleged offending quite often trumps an individual's status as an actual trafficked person. Those of us representing individuals implicated in county lines operations, remembering that frequently the distinction between perpetrator and victim is very fine, have seen this play out in an increasing number of cases. The s.45 defence will be available to a credible victim of exploitation if charged with some typical county lines offences such as drug supply, possession of a bladed article / offensive weapon and money laundering but not allegations of human trafficking or possession of firearms.

Legal professionals will know that often the only option available to victims of exploitation charged with excluded offences is to invite the CPS not to prosecute in accordance with the stage 4 public interest test, which applies to all allegations of criminal behaviour (see discussion in chapter 13).

Elements of the s.45 defence

The elements of the defence under s.45 are subject to the age of the individual at the time of the alleged offence. There is one statutory test for those under 18 years old and a separate statutory test for those 18 years or older. The Court of Appeal has repeatedly emphasised the importance of all legal professionals understanding that the legislation created two regimes of "*critical difference*" (see *R v ADG* [2023] EWCA Crim 1309 at para 39)

Adults

Under s.45(1) to (3), for an individual 18 years old or over at the time of the alleged offence, the following questions apply:

- Did the individual do the act constituting the offence because they were compelled to do it by either another person or by the individual's circumstances?

- Was the compulsion <u>attributable</u> to slavery or a direct consequence of the individual being, or having been, a victim of slavery or a victim of human trafficking?

- Would a reasonable person in the <u>same situation</u> as the individual and having the individual's <u>relevant characteristics</u> have had no realistic alternative to doing the act?

<u>'Compelled'</u>

The term 'compelled' is well established having been set out in the 'non-punishment' principles of Article 26 of the Council of Europe Convention on Action against Trafficking in Human Beings and Article 8 of the EU Anti-Trafficking Directive 2011/36/EU. The Explanatory Note attached to the Convention interprets the term 'compelled' as follows:

> "*...the requirement that victims have been compelled to be involved in unlawful activities shall be understood as compromising, at a minimum, victims that have been subject to any of the illicit means referred to in Article 4 (definition of trafficking), when such involvement results from compulsion*"

The Court of Appeal in *AAD* [2022] EWCA Crim 106 was recently tasked with considering whether the term 'compelled' had the same meaning as 'causation'. The issue was whether the approach should be that of causation, specifically whether the offence had been caused by the traffickers, or the more restrictive interpretation of compulsion. The Court of Appeal decided on the more restrictive interpretation. Lord Justice Fulford, providing the judgment on behalf of the Court, stated at para 145:

> "*We are unable to accept this argument. The starting point is the statutory language which is entirely clear: the terms of the section 45 defence require that the person was "compelled" to do the act, that the*

> *"compulsion" is attributable to slavery or to relevant exploitation and that a reasonable person in the same situation would have had no realistic alternative. The intention of Parliament could not have been clearer: compulsion and causation self-evidently have entirely different meanings and the legislature decided to adopt the approach of the former. Not only is this the express domestic legislative requirement but it coincides with United Kingdom's international obligations."*

Lord Justice Fulford went on to set out the wording of the various international definitions and the resulting obligations placed upon the United Kingdom. It was his view that the wording of s.45 aptly reflected the obligations and that there was "*no sustainable foundation for the submission that this legislative provision should be reformulated in the manner suggested*" and that any such attempt would "*involve the wholesale rewriting of a statutory defence without any, or any material, justification*" (para 153).

'Attributable'

As already outlined, there is no blanket immunity from prosecution for victims of trafficking. The inclusion of the attribution requirement means that there will need to be some evidence of a nexus between the trafficking and the criminal act.

For a helpful illustration of the attribution requirement in practice, legal professionals may want to consider the recent Court of Appeal decision in *BLS* [2022] EWCA Crim 1079.

The defendant in BLS had been arrested in a car parked outside a cannabis factory. He had a key to the premises in his possession and £100 in his wallet. There was a knife in the driver's door pocket. In the house police found large amounts of cash and three mobile telephones. The defendant told police that he was paid £200 per week by the people who hired him and his duties only involved looking after the plants. He had also been given the car by the people who paid him for watering the plants. He said he entered the UK illegally 2 years earlier and was only

16 years of age, although it was later revealed that he was 19 years old. In interview the defendant told police that he had lived rough until he met a man who had offered him the job of looking after the plants. He lived at the house and met the man at McDonald's once a week for payment.

The defendant pleaded guilty in the Crown Court to production of cannabis and possession of the knife. He waived privilege for the appeal and his previous solicitors confirmed that he had not provided instructions consistent with him having been a victim of slavery. The Court of Appeal was aware that in mitigation his legal representative stated that he had been *"exploited because of his vulnerable position and was probably quite easily persuaded to take up the position that he was offered"* (para 10). However, the judge had rejected that submission stating:

> *"I don't think he took any persuasion at all. I think he was perfectly happy to play the role which he did because it helped protect him against the risk of detention and deportation. That is why he lied about his age when he was arrested."*

The Court of Appeal took a similar approach to the appeal, which was based on the submission that the defendant had subsequently been the subject of a conclusive grounds decision by the SCA that he was the victim of trafficking. In her judgment at paragraphs 32 to 33, Mrs Justice McGovern stated:

> *"32. Even if we were to accept the applicant's case about being trafficked from Vietnam (and it is not necessary to come to a final conclusion on that), we have no hesitation in finding that there was no nexus between the applicant's being trafficked into the UK and his carrying out his function as a cannabis gardener. This is because at the time of his arrest the applicant had £100 on his person; on the day of his arrest he also had access to at least £600-700 in cash found in the house; he had a key to the house and could come and go as he pleased; he had a car which he could drive in which he kept a knife, and he was not under supervision. These facts are not consistent with a person*

> *being compelled to act for the purposes of trafficking or slavery. Whatever the history of the applicant's journey to the UK (and as indicated it is not necessary to make findings about that), it is apparent that by the time of his arrest the applicant was not the subject of compulsion.*
>
> *33. He could have left at any time. He gave an account of events which was not credible and did not discharge any evidential burden on him. We also find that no reasonable adult, sharing his characteristics, would have been left with no reasonable alternative but to act in the way he did."*

The Court of Appeal found that the defendant's involvement in cannabis production was not attributable to his apparent human trafficking. Significant importance was placed on his ability to leave the premises, his access to money and the absence of constant supervision. Legal professionals working in the area of county lines will understand the significance of such a narrow approach being adopted on the issue of attribution, particularly given the significant periods of time that can pass from initial recruitment to police intervention.

<u>'Same Situation' and 'Relevant Characteristics'</u>

Under s.45(5), relevant characteristics are defined as "*age, sex and any physical or mental illness or disability*". This mirrors the common law position in relation to duress. This is a provision in the context of county lines cases. As already discussed, the drugs gangs frequently target and recruit vulnerable adults to undertake specific roles. This provision allows the jury to be directed to consider those vulnerabilities, provided they relate to one of the specific areas set out.

The question may be asked about whether a "*reasonable person in the same situation*" should adopt the individual's experience of having been a victim of human trafficking. The point is addressed in the *Crown Court Compendium Part I (July 2024)* at 18-30. In short although a 'reasonable person' is a fixed objective standard in criminal proceedings, the inclusion of the term "*same situation*" would allow the jury to assess what a reasonable person would have done if they had shared the individual's trafficking circumstances when committing the act.

Children

Under s.45(4), for an individual under 18 years old at the time of the alleged offence, the following questions apply:

- Did the individual do the act as a direct consequence of the individual being, or having been, a victim of slavery or a victim of human trafficking?

- Would a reasonable person in the same situation as the individual and having the individual's relevant characteristics have done the act?

The first point to note in relation to children is that compulsion does not feature. In *ADG* [2023] EWCA Crim 1309, convictions were quashed after the jury were wrongly directed to look for compulsion with defendants who were under 18 years old at the time of the alleged offences.

The second point to note is the absence of the adult "*no realistic alternative*" requirement when considering whether a reasonable person would have acted like the child. In the case of an individual under 18, the legislation simply requires that a reasonable person in the same situation and with the child's relevant characteristics would do what the child did.

Legal professionals are strongly advised to have a full understanding of the distinction between the adult and child provisions given the significant difference in the requirements placed upon the defence.

Burden of Proof

The MSA 2015 does not explicitly state where the burden of proof lies when considering the statutory defence under s.45.

The answer was provided by the Court of Appeal in *MK* [2018] EWCA Crim 667. In that case the prosecution successfully persuaded the trial judge that there was a reverse burden; the defence had the legal burden of proving all elements of the defence on the balance of probabilities, with the exception of whether the defendant was a victim of trafficking or slavery. The Court of Appeal disagreed and decided if all limbs of the defence were raised in the evidence it would be for the prosecution to prove beyond reasonable doubt that one of more of the limbs would not apply. As confirmed by Lord Burnett, the then Lord Chief Justice, at paragraph 45:

> *"Section 45 of the 2015 Act does not bear the interpretation urged by the prosecution upon, and accepted by, the judges below. It does not implicitly require the defendant to bear the legal or persuasive burden of proof of any element of the defence. The burden on a defendant is evidential. It is for the defendant to raise evidence of each of those elements and for the prosecution to disprove one or more of them to the criminal standard in the usual way".*

The decision in *MK* to place the burden of proof upon the prosecution has been relied upon by the Court of Appeal in more recent decisions to restrict the scope of the s.45 defence (see for example the comments of Lord Justice Fulford at paragraph 154 of the judgment in *AAD* when refusing to equate the terms causation and compelled).

CHAPTER THIRTEEN

IS IT IN THE PUBLIC INTEREST TO PROSECUTE?

Overview of 'public interest' in human trafficking cases

The fourth and final stage of the CPS four stage test requires a consideration of whether there would be a public interest in prosecuting a credible victim of human trafficking.

The 'public interest' test must be carefully considered in all cases where there is a credible victim of human trafficking. It must be considered in cases where there is no clear evidence of duress i.e. where the answer to stage 2 is negative. It must be considered in cases where there is no clear evidence of the elements necessary for the application of the statutory defence under s.45 i.e. where the answer to stage 3 is negative. As outlined in chapter 12, significantly the public interest test must be satisfied even where individuals are charged with offences listed in schedule 4 of the MSA 2015 and therefore not covered by the s.45 statutory defence e.g. human trafficking and possession of firearms.

The CPS has the final decision when it comes to a determination of the public interest test. Prosecutors are required to consider and apply the factors listed in the Code for Crown Prosecutors, but with specific consideration of the following:

- the seriousness of the offence
- the level of culpability of the suspect
- the harm caused to the victim

- the suspect's age and maturity

As touched upon in other chapters of this practical guide, it is notable and significant that the first factor listed relates not to the individual but to the alleged offence.

Following the decision of the Court of Appeal in *VSJ* [2017] EWCA Crim 36, in cases where stage 2 and stage 3 have been answered in the negative for adults, prosecutors are also required to consider (para 20):

- Whether there is a nexus or connection between the trafficking/slavery or past trafficking/slavery and the alleged offending; and, if so,

- Whether the force of compulsion from the trafficking/slavery or past trafficking/slavery acting on the suspect is enough to remove their culpability/criminality or reduce their culpability/criminality to a point where it is not in the public interest to prosecute them.

The test is necessarily different in cases where stage 2 and stage 3 have been answered in the negative for children as there is no need for compulsion. Therefore, the Court of Appeal in VSJ stated that prosecutors should consider (para 35):

- whether there is a nexus or connection between the trafficking/slavery or past trafficking/slavery and the alleged offending; and, if so,

- whether the circumstances remove the child's culpability/criminality or reduce it to a point where it is not in the public interest to prosecute them. If there was compulsion, then this will reduce the public interest, but it is not a necessary element. As for an adult, the more serious the offence, the stronger the mitigating factors will need to be before it is not in the public interest to prosecute.

Legal professionals working in this area will know that a CPS decision not to prosecute in a case where there is no clear evidence supporting either duress or the s.45 statutory defence are extremely rare.

Challenging a CPS decision to prosecute before MSA 2015

As outlined in chapter 12, before the MSA 2015 was passed in Parliament there was no statutory defence. Therefore, legal representatives seeking to challenge a CPS decision to prosecute a credible victim of human trafficking were forced to seek a stay of the indictment as an abuse of process in accordance with the second limb expounded in *R v Horseferry Road Magistrates Court ex parte Bennett [1994] 1 AC 42,* to the broad effect that it would be unfair and oppressive to put the defendant on trial.

The existence of the abuse of process jurisdiction in the context of trafficking cases before the introduction of the MSA 2015 was acknowledged in several Court of Appeal authorities. In *N and L* [2012] EWCA Crim 189, Lord Judge, the then Lord Chief Justice, giving the judgment of the Court stated (para 21):

> *"Summarising the essential principles, the implementation of the UK's Convention obligation is normally achieved by the proper exercise of the long established prosecutorial discretion which enables the CPS, however strong the evidence may be, to decide that it would be inappropriate to proceed or to continue with the prosecution of a defendant who is unable to advance duress as a defence but who falls within the protective ambit of article 26. This requires a judgment to be made by the CPS in the individual case in the light of all the available evidence. That responsibility is vested not in the court but in the prosecuting authority. The court may intervene in an individual case if its process is abused by using the "ultimate sanction" of a stay of the proceedings. The burden of showing that the process is being or has been abused on the basis of the improper exercise of the prosecutorial discretion rests on the defendant."*

Lord Judge went on in the case of *R v L* [2013] EWCA Crim 991 to reiterate the point, emphasising that the Court "*protects the right of the victim of trafficking by overseeing the decision of the prosecutor and refuses to countenance any prosecution which fails to acknowledge and address the victim's subservient situation*" (para 16). The availability of the abuse of process for cases before the introduction of the MSA 2015 was further approved by the Court of Appeal in the decisions of *VSJ* and S(G) [2018] EWCA Crim 1824.

Challenging a CPS decision to prosecute after MSA 2015

The question that was asked after the passing of the MSA 2015 was whether the CPS decision to prosecute was still subject to the abuse of process jurisdiction.

The Court of Appeal initially answered in the negative. In the cases of *DS* [2020] EWCA Crim 285 and *A* [2020] EWCA Crim 1408, the Court of Appeal stated that the enactment of the MSA 2015 meant that it was for the jury to decide the facts relevant to whether an individual's exploitation provided a defence under s.45 and that proceedings should only be stayed if a conventional abuse of process was found. In *DS*, Lord Burnett, the then Lord Chief Justice, gave the judgment of the Court and stated (para 40):

> *"In our judgment, the result of the enactment of the 2015 Act and the section 45 statutory defence is that the responsibility for deciding the facts relevant to the status of DS as a Victim of Trafficking is unquestionably that of the jury. Formerly, there was a lacuna in that regard, which the courts sought to fill by expanding somewhat the notion of abuse of process, which required the Judge to make relevant decisions of fact. That is no longer necessary, and cases to which the 2015 Act applies should proceed on the basis that they will be stayed if, but only if, an abuse of process as conventionally defined is found. By way of summary only, this involves two categories of abuse, as is well known. The first is that a fair trial is not possible and the second is that*

it would be wrong to try the defendant because of some misconduct by the state in bringing about the prosecution. Neither of these species of abuse affected this case, and it should not therefore have been stayed."

The issue was revisited by the Court of Appeal in the recent decision of *AAD* [2022] EWCA Crim 106. Somewhat surprisingly, the Court overruled the previous authorities and stated that the previously identified 'special category of abuse' in human trafficking cases still applied for criminal offences committed after the introduction of the MSA 2015. In doing so the Court expressed itself "*rather puzzled*" by some of the observations of Lord Burnett in DS (para 125). Lord Justice Fulford, handing down the judgment on behalf of the Court, stated (para 127):

"We are also a little wary of the reference in [44] of the judgment in DS to an arguable abuse of process "properly so called". We accept that abuse of process applications of the kind made in M(L), L(C) and N and L have their own features. But, as will be gathered, we consider that is essentially so just because of the special context and features of VOT cases and of the international obligations relating to VOTs. The underpinning, however, for such an application to stay remains that of unfairness and oppression and illegality: which is a conventional underpinning for any typical limb two abuse application. And if there has been an unjustified and material failure to have regard to CPS guidance in this kind of context or an irrational and perverse departure from a conclusive grounds decision in this kind of context then an arguable case of unfairness and oppression and illegality would potentially be there."

Lord Justice Fulford unsurprisingly emphasised that a decision to stay the indictment would only be "*exercised in very limited circumstances*" (para 115), before going on to explain in full why an abuse of process argument ought to be available for offences committed after the passing of the MSA 2015 (paras 116 to 118):

"116. At first sight, and absent authority to the contrary, it is difficult to see why it should not. Clearly the 2015 Act was designed to improve the position of VOTs (or those claiming to be VOTs) by providing for the opportunity, in certain kinds of cases, to raise a substantive defence: which, if raised on a sufficient evidential basis, it would then be for the prosecution to disprove to the criminal standard. There is, on the face of it, no incompatibility in such a defence being available and there also being available the potential (in an exceptional case) for advancing the abuse of process jurisdiction with regard to a decision to prosecute and pursue to trial. Indeed, to retain the availability of the abuse of process jurisdiction for this purpose would seem better to preserve the obligations in the Convention and Directive, which extend not only to VOTs not being punished but also, in appropriate cases, to not being prosecuted.

117. Moreover, although the abuse of process jurisdiction in this context has sometimes been described as "special" or "unusual" that is, in our judgment, only really so, in substance, just because of the context…After all, any abuse of process argument has to take into account the context: and here such context necessarily includes the international obligations relating to VOTs and to the very sensitive issues arising with regard to VOTs.

118. Such a view in no way would, in our judgment, subvert the provisions of or purpose of the 2015 Act. Rather, it would complement them and supplement them. Nor does the availability of the abuse of process jurisdiction give alleged VOTs carte blanche to circumvent a prosecution. We emphasise: a decision to prosecute is for the CPS, not for the courts. Further, where the facts are in dispute then it is for a jury to determine those facts. It thus will be fruitless for a defendant to seek to avoid prosecution by alleging (truthfully or not) status as a VOT or (even where such status of VOT is admitted) by disputing the asserted lack of nexus between that status and the criminality in question. It will be fruitless just because those matters will be jury matters."

Lord Justice Fulford went on to state that there would be no basis for any such abuse of process challenge if the CPS were able to show that it had considered the relevant prosecutorial guidance and provided a rational basis for departing from a conclusive grounds decision of the SCA (para 119). A simple disagreement about the decision to prosecute of itself will never suffice. However, Lord Justice Fulford stated a failure of the CPS to either consider the guidance or to provide no rational basis for departing from the conclusive grounds decision – something he thought "*highly improbable*" given the greater awareness these days of trafficking – may, in principle, be found irrational and result in a stay of the indictment.

The judgment of the Court of Appeal in *AAD* confirmed that the second limb of the abuse of process jurisdiction remains available in principle in all cases where there is a credible victim of human trafficking, including those charged with offences listed in Schedule 4 of the MSA 2015. There is nothing particularly 'special' about the category of abuse as the core requirements of unfairness, oppression and illegality remain central to the applications; it remains in place to protect credible victims from poor policy decisions by prosecutors. For a rare example of a conviction being found unsafe by the Court of Appeal because of a CPS failure to follow its own guidance on the prosecution of human trafficking victims see *AFU* [2023] EWCA Crim 23. However, those of us working in this area know that these cases are rare and there is no risk at all of any opening of the floodgates.

PART FOUR

SENTENCING IN COUNTY LINES CASES

CHAPTER FOURTEEN

SENTENCING PRINCIPLES IN 'COUNTY LINES' CASES

Legal professionals working in this area will be aware of the maximum sentences and relevant guidelines applicable to the typical county lines offences of human trafficking, drug supply, money laundering and possession of weapons. When tasked with considering appeals against sentence in county lines cases the Court of Appeal has typically taken a tough stance with appellants, particularly those shown to have been involved in the organisation and management of exploited individuals.

The tough approach was exemplified in *R v Mohammed (Zakaria)* [2019] EWCA Crim 1881. The case concerned offences of drug supply, for which the appellant had been sentenced to 6 years imprisonment, and human trafficking, for which the appellant had been sentenced to a consecutive period of 8 years imprisonment. In that case three children had been taken from Birmingham, housed in poor quality accommodation in Lincoln and used to supply drugs in a large-scale county lines operation.

The Court of Appeal started by making it clear that it would not in "*any way shrink from the fact that a man who becomes involved in offending such as this, even if he does not play a leading role, must recognise that he is involved in very serious criminality*" and that there must be an expectation of "*condign punishment*" (para 32). Although it allowed part of the appeal due to the appellant's youth, good record and personal background, the Court stated that the sentencing judge was entitled to impose consecutive offences as offences under the MSA 2015 were "*distinct, with separate elements requiring separate recognition*" (para 41). To emphasise the seriousness with which these offences should and would be treated, the Court of Appeal concluded "*these were very grave offences. Anybody who becomes involved in such offending will receive a long sentence by deterrence*" (para 46).

As legal professionals working in the area of county lines will know from personal experience, the decision in *Mohammed (Zakaria)* is routinely relied upon to justify the imposition of lengthy, consecutive prison sentences where individuals are convicted of both drug supply and human trafficking offences; often the main submission of the defence advocate will be to invite the judge to have regard for the totality principle and reduce the lengthy overall sentence.

The Court of Appeal has followed up that tough rhetoric with tough decisions.

In *R v Nixon* [2021] EW CA Crim 575 the Court of Appeal increased the sentence imposed upon the defendants by the sentencing judge following a reference by the Attorney General. The defendant in that case was involved in a county lines operation supplying both crack cocaine and heroin between London and Devon. The operation also involved arranging for four children to be transported from London to Devon to work as drug runners. The sentencing judge decided that the drugs offences merited 3 years 4 months imprisonment and the human trafficking offences merited 4 years 6 months, with the total sentence being 7 years imprisonment after a reduction for totality. The Court of Appeal agreed with the Attorney General that the individual sentences for the offences were too short; instead it should have been 4 years for the drug supply and 7 years for the human trafficking. Therefore, the sentence was increased after consideration of totality to 10 years imprisonment.

In *R v Mason* [2023] EWCA Crim 1540 the Court of Appeal took a similarly tough stance when concluding that a sentence uplift of only 12 months was insufficient to account for human trafficking as part of a drug supply operation. At paragraph 53 of the judgment, Lord Justice Popplewell stated:

> *"Many of the children were particularly vulnerable for the reasons we have described. They were controlled by fear of serious violence and forced unwillingly to work in this trade. They were not merely encouraged or enticed to do so, but forcibly exploited by compulsion. That had particularly serious consequences in a number of ways. It enabled the operators of the line to run the county lines business remotely. County lines drug dealing is a scourge of modern society, with all the misery it inflicts, and any criminality which facilitates it is for that reason alone serious. But, more importantly, the effect on the young victims of the Modern Slavery Act offences themselves was also very serious. They were encouraged to become drug users so as to become embroiled in a way which made it difficult to remove themselves from the trade. They were put in fear of violence from the county line operation itself... They were put in danger, moreover, of violence from others in the drugs and gang world in which they were forced to work. They were isolated from the efforts of social services and other services to promote their welfare. They were put at serious risk of becoming entrenched in that world, even after this operation ceased, in a way from which they might find it difficult to escape. This is all serious enough if it happens to adults, but it is particularly so when it involves vulnerable children and young people, as young as 14 and 15."*

The message for those involved in county lines operations is very clear. If you involve yourself in county lines, even if you are not at the top of the management chain, and you are convicted of both drug supply and human trafficking offences, you should expect a lengthy prison sentence. The significant impact this approach will have on young or vulnerable individuals at the lower end of the management chain was exemplified in the case of *R v Ogunjimi* [2019] EWCA Crim 201.

The defendant in *Ogunjimi*, when still only 17 years old, pleaded guilty to a single offence of conspiracy to supply class A drugs as part of a county lines operation. He was 16 years old at start of the conspiracy. He was based in Huntingdon, in regular contact with the controller of the drugs lined based in London, described as a 'soldier' for the operation in text messages and had his travel booked for him by the controller of the drugs line. The prosecution described the young defendant as having carried out a principal role. In his pre-sentence report the defendant described the debt bondage used to recruit him and the control that was subsequently exercised over him by older men. The author of the pre-sentence report described him as naïve and immature. Nevertheless, the Court of Appeal concluded (para 28):

> *"In a case such as this, where the appellant has, for a number of weeks at least, encountered the victims of drug abuse day in and day out and persisted in supplying them with Class A drugs in exchange for money, it would not be reasonable to conclude that the appellant's youth diminished his appreciation of the damage he was involved in doing to any substantial extent"*

The reasoning and conclusions of the Court of Appeal in these cases provides clear guidance for those representing individuals who may have been recruited through exploitation but have nevertheless found themselves convicted of criminal offences. The Court of Appeal is unlikely to be of assistance.

CHAPTER FIFTEEN

ANCILLARY ORDERS IN 'COUNTY LINES' CASES

Confiscation

The Proceeds of Crime Act 2002 created a single model for confiscation following conviction in criminal cases to enable the recovery of the proceeds of crime. The confiscation regime is severe and unforgiving for defendants. Any offence where a defendant has benefited financially from criminal activity can be the subject of confiscation proceedings.

The Court of Appeal in *Whittington* [2010] 1 Cr. App. R. (S) 545 provided the following useful guide to practitioners:

- Step 1 – the confiscation process starts either when the prosecution asks for it or when the Court believes it would be appropriate.

- Step 2 – the judge must decide whether the defendant has a 'criminal lifestyle'. This will depend solely upon the nature of the offence for which the defendant has been convicted but would automatically cover offences of human trafficking, drug supply and money laundering (although not s.329) which are listed in schedule 2 of POCA 2002.

- Step 3 – the judge must decide whether the defendant has benefited from criminal conduct. If found to have a criminal lifestyle, which will almost always be the case in county lines prosecutions, the Court will consider whether the defendant has benefited from "*general criminal conduct*", undertaking an unlimited historical inquiry i.e. all of the defendant's criminal conduct regardless of when it occurred may be included in the assessment.

- Step 4 – the judge must determine the gross market value of the defendant's financial benefit, referred to as the 'recoverable amount'. In criminal lifestyle cases this is calculated by applying the relevant statutory assumptions – what has been received, what has been retained and what has been spent is deemed to be criminal benefit – unless either there would be a serious risk of injustice or the defendant is able to show that an assumption is incorrect.

- Step 5 – the judge must make a confiscation order in the sum of the 'recoverable amount' unless the defendant is able to prove that all existing assets are less than that amount, referred to as 'the available amount'.

Confiscation proceedings frequently follow county lines prosecutions, particularly if law enforcement has been able to identify and successfully prosecute those higher up the management chain. The exploited individuals, if convicted by a jury of any of the relevant offences, rarely find themselves the subject of confiscation proceedings given their inevitable lack of financial resources or available assets.

Forfeiture

Following convictions the sentencing judge has several powers available to order forfeiture of items from defendants.

Under s.153 of the Sentencing Act 2020, the Court has a general power to deprive defendants of property in their possession or under their control at the time of arrest where it had been used or was intended to be used for committing or facilitating any criminal offence. This will frequently cover mobile telephones, computers and vehicles.

Such orders should only be made in straightforward cases involving unencumbered property (*Troth* [1980] Crim LR 249); if there are third party interests in the property it would likely not be appropriate to make such an order as they may be the subject of civil proceedings.

The Court is required to approach the issue with proportionality in mind. Forfeiture should not be ordered if it would cause the defendant undue hardship and the judge ought to have regard to the totality of sentence. In *Buddo* (1982) 4 Cr. App. R. S. 268, the sentencing judge had ordered the deprivation of the defendant's caravan in addition to imposing an immediate term of imprisonment for burglary offences. The Court of Appeal overturned the decision stating that the deprivation order added "*greatly to the severity of the sentence*" and it was "*overdoing the punishment to make the order*" (page 270).

Legal professionals representing individuals convicted in county lines cases will need to be alert to these issues and prepared to challenge broad, sweeping applications by the prosecution at the conclusion of the sentencing hearing.

The Court may make similar forfeiture orders under specific provisions relevant to the offences for which the defendant has been convicted. For example, s.11 of the MSA 2015 allows the Court to order forfeiture of a vehicle, boat or aircraft used to commit a human trafficking offence under section 2 of that Act and s.27 of the MDA 1971 allows the Court to order forfeiture of "*anything shown to the satisfaction of the Court to relate to the offence*" committed under that Act.

Slavery and Trafficking Prevention Orders

Under s.14 of the MSA 2015, the Court may make a Slavery and Trafficking Prevention Order ('STPO') following conviction for an offence listed in Schedule 1, which includes the human trafficking offences covered in sections 2 and 4. Such an order may also be made on application (s.15 MSA 2015).

Before making such an order the Court must be satisfied that there is a risk that the defendant may commit a slavery or human trafficking offence and that it is necessary to make the order to protect persons generally, or particular persons, from the physical or psychological harm which would be likely to occurred if the defendant committed such an offence (s.14(2)).

The Court of Appeal in *Wabelua* [2020] EWCA Crim 783 provided guidance as to the legal principles applicable to the imposition of an STPO, specifically (para 36):

> *"As subsection (2) makes clear, an order can only be made if the court is satisfied that there is a risk that the defendant may commit a slavery or human trafficking offence and satisfied that the order is necessary for the purpose of protecting persons generally, or particular persons, from the physical or psychological harm which would be likely to occur if the defendant committed such an offence. The subsection does not require the court to apply any particular standard of proof.*
>
> *(b) Although an STPO is a civil order, breach of it carries a serious criminal sanction. The risk that the defendant may commit a slavery or human trafficking offence must therefore be real, not remote, and must be sufficient to justify the making of such an order. In considering whether such a risk is present in a particular case, the court is entitled to have regard to all the information before it, including in relation to any previous convictions of the defendant concerned, or in relation to any previous failure to comply with court orders.*
>
> *(c) The order must be necessary for the purpose of protecting persons generally, or particular persons, from the physical or psychological harm which would be likely to occur if the defendant committed a further slavery or human trafficking offence, and not merely desirable or helpful in that regard.*
>
> *(d) In many cases where the risk is identified, there will also be a necessity to make an order. However, they are distinct preconditions to*

the making of an order and they require separate consideration. In determining whether any order is necessary, the court must consider whether the risk is sufficiently addressed by the nature and length of the sentence imposed, and/or the presence of other controls on the defendant, and/or the important ability of a Chief Officer of Police to apply for an order if it becomes necessary to do so at some time in the future.

(e) The criterion of necessity applies not only to the making of an order at all, but also to the individual terms of the order where one is necessary.

(f) The terms of the order must in addition be both reasonable and proportionate to the purpose for which it is made: that is one of the reasons why the court must first have made a clear assessment as to why an order is necessary. The court should take into account any adverse effect of the order on the defendant's rehabilitation, and the realities of life in an age of electronic means of communication.

(g) The terms of the order must be clear, so that the defendant can readily understand what he is prohibited from doing and those responsible for enforcing the order can readily identify any breach.

(h) A draft order must be provided to the court and to all defence advocates in good time to enable its terms to be considered before the sentencing hearing. We recognise the pressures on judges and advocates, and we recognise that the sentencing process may follow immediately after the jury's verdicts. However, the necessary careful consideration cannot be given to the proposed order if the draft is produced at the last moment."

The prohibitions imposed on a defendant by an STPO must be tailored to the role they played. The explanatory notes that accompanied the MSA 2015 set out examples of the type of prohibitions that may be imposed, such as "*preventing a person from participating in a particular type of business, operating as a gangmaster, visiting a particular place, working with children or travelling to a specified country*" (para 80).

The terms of the STPO may extend to a prohibition on foreign travel (s.18) or a requirement for a defendant to provide identified individuals with their name and address (s.19).

The STPO must be imposed for a fixed period of at least 5 years or until further order (s.17(4)).

An interim STPO may be made where an application for an STPO has been made under s.15 and the Court considers "*it just to do so*" (s.21(3)). An interim order may only be made for a specified, fixed period and will cease to have effect once the main application has been determined by the Court.

An appeal against the imposition of an STPO following conviction or interim STPO will follow the same process as an appeal against sentence (s.22).

A breach of either an STPO or interim STPO without a reasonable excuse would amount to a criminal offence (s.30(1)). The maximum sentence is 6 months imprisonment or a fine or both on summary conviction of 5 years imprisonment following conviction on indictment (s.30(3)).

Slavery and Trafficking Risk Orders

Under s.23 MSA 2015, the Magistrates' Court may make a Slavery and Trafficking Risk Order ('STRO') on the application of a Chief officer of Police, an immigration officer or the Director General of the National Crime Agency.

The test for making an STRO is set out at s.23(2), namely that the Court must be satisfied that there is a risk that the individual may commit a slavery or human trafficking offence and that it is necessary to make an STRO for the purpose of protecting persons generally, or particular persons, from physical or psychological harm which would be likely to occur if the individual committed such an offence.

There is no requirement with an STRO that the person in respect of whom an order is sought has previously been convicted or cautioned in relation to a criminal offence.

As with STPOs the prohibitions within the STRO are a matter for the Court applying the same principles and statutory test. The terms of the STRO may extend to a prohibition on foreign travel (s.25) or a requirement for the individual to provide identified individuals with their name and address (s.26).

An interim STRO may be made where an application for an STRO has been made under s.23 and the Court considers "*it just to do so*" (s.28(3)). An interim order may only be made for a specified, fixed period and will cease to have effect once the main application has been determined by the Court.

An appeal against the making of an STRO or an interim STRO will follow the same process as an appeal against sentence from the Magistrates' Court to the Crown Court (s.29(3)). The Crown Court considering an appeal may make such orders as are "*necessary*" to give effect to the determination of the appeal.

A breach of either an STRO or interim STRO without a reasonable excuse would amount to a criminal offence (s.30(1)). The maximum sentence is 6 months imprisonment or a fine or both on summary conviction of 5 years imprisonment following conviction on indictment (s.30(3)).

Serious Crime Prevention Orders

Under s.19 of the Serious Crime Act 2007, the Crown Court may make a Serious Crime Prevention Order ('SCPO') if it has reasonable grounds to believe that the order would protect the public by preventing, restricting or disrupting involvement by that person in serious crime. The provision applies to an individual either convicted in the Magistrates' Court of having committed a serious offence and then committed to the Crown Court for sentence or convicted in the Crown Court of a serious offence.

A 'serious offence' would include convictions for supplying drugs, human trafficking (both s.2 and s.4), money laundering (including s.329) and several firearms offences.

The SCPO provides the Court with a broader range of options for imposing restrictions and requirements upon defendants than STPOs and STROs. However, the Court of Appeal has made it clear that a proportionate approach must be taken and the terms of the order must be commensurate with the risk (*R v Hancox* [2010] EWCA Crim 102 at para 10). Furthermore, the Court stated that the terms of the order must be "*practicable and enforceable and satisfying the test of precision and certainty*" given the potential consequences of breaching the terms (para 11).

The SCPO cannot be in force for more than 5 years (s.16(2))

An appeal against the decision to impose or vary/not vary an SCPO is made to the Court Appeal (s.24).

A breach of the SCPO without a reasonable excuse would amount to a criminal offence (s.25). The maximum sentence is 12 months imprisonment or a fine or both on summary conviction, or 5 years imprisonment or a fine following conviction on indictment.

Sexual Harm Prevention Order

Sections 343 to 358 of the Sentencing Act 2020 provide the power to impose a Sexual Harm Prevention Order ('SHPO') upon defendants convicted of not only some sexual offences but also non-sexual offences. For example, an offence of human trafficking contrary to s.2 of the MSA 2015 is covered under schedule 5 of the SOA 2003.

The only prohibitions that may be included in the order are those which are necessary to protect the public from sexual harm from the offender or to protect children or vulnerable adults from sexual harm from the offender outside the UK (s.343(2)).

The leading authority on the imposition of an SHPO remains *Smith (Steve)* [2011] EWCA Crim 1772. In that judgment the Court of Appeal set out the three key questions when deciding whether to impose such an order:

- Is the making of a SHPO necessary to protect the public from sexual harm through the commission of scheduled offences?

- If some order is necessary are the terms imposed nevertheless oppressive?

- Overall are the terms proportionate?

Legal professionals served with such applications ought to be prepared to challenge the often broad, sweeping provisions put forward by the prosecution. For example, in *Bolton* [2010] EWCA Crim 1177, the Court of Appeal stated that an SHPO would not be appropriate because it was unnecessary alongside the indefinite prison sentence imposed. Legal professionals must approach the question carefully and reflect upon the sentence imposed along with any other orders.

The Court of Appeal in *Smith* made it clear that although SHPOs are preventative it does not follow that anything is permissible, stating "*it is not legitimate to impose multiple prohibitions on a defendant just in case he commits a different kind of offence. There must be an identifiable risk... before this kind of prohibition can be justified*" (para 22).

An appeal against the imposition of an SHPO will follow the same process as an appeal against sentence (s.53 SA 2020).

A breach of an SHPO without a reasonable excuse would amount to a criminal offence (s.354 SA 2020). The maximum sentence is 6 months imprisonment or a fine or both on summary conviction, or 5 years imprisonment or a fine following conviction on indictment.

'The Electronic Communications Code: A Practical Guide – Second Edition' by Kerry Bretherton KC, James Castle, Mark Loveday
'A Practical Guide to the Independent School Standards – September 2023 Edition' by Sarah McKimm
'A Practical Guide to Estate Administration and Crypto Assets' by Richard Marshall
'A Practical Guide to Parental Alienation in Private and Public Law Children Cases' by Sam King QC & Frankie Shama
'Contested Heritage – Removing Art from Land and Historic Buildings' by Richard Harwood QC, Catherine Dobson, David Sawtell
'The Limits of Separate Legal Personality: When Those Running a Company Can Be Held Personally Liable for Losses Caused to Third Parties Outside of the Company' by Dr Mike Wilkinson
'A Practical Guide to Transgender Law' by Robin Moira White & Nicola Newbegin
'A Practical Guide to 'Stranded Spouses' in Family Law' by Mani Singh Basi
'A Practical Guide to Residential Freehold Conveyancing' by Lorraine Richardson
'A Practical Guide to Pensions on Divorce for Lawyers' by Bryan Scant
'A Practical Guide to Challenging Sham Marriage Allegations in Immigration Law' by Priya Solanki
'A Practical Guide to Digital Communications Evidence in Criminal Law' by Sam Willis
'A Practical Guide to Legal Rights in Scotland' by Sarah-Jane Macdonald
'A Practical Guide to New Build Conveyancing' by Paul Sams & Rebecca East
'A Practical Guide to Inherited Wealth on Divorce' by Hayley Trim
'A Practical Guide to Practice Direction 12J and Domestic Abuse in Private Law Children Proceedings' by Rebecca Cross & Malvika Jaganmohan
'A Practical Guide to Confiscation and Restraint' by Narita Bahra QC, John Carl Townsend, David Winch
'A Practical Guide to the Law of Forests in Scotland' by Philip Buchan
'A Practical Guide to Health and Medical Cases in Immigration Law' by Rebecca Chapman & Miranda Butler
'A Practical Guide to Bad Character Evidence for Criminal Practitioners by Aparna Rao
'A Practical Guide to Extradition Law post-Brexit' by Myles Grandison et al
'A Practical Guide to Hoarding and Mental Health for Housing Lawyers' by Rachel Coyle

'Stephens on Contractual Indemnities' by Richard Stephens
'A Practical Guide to the EU Succession Regulation' by Richard Frimston
'A Practical Guide to Solicitor and Client Costs – Second Edition' by Robin Dunne
'Constructive Dismissal – Practice Pointers and Principles' by Benjimin Burgher
'A Practical Guide to Religion and Belief Discrimination Claims in the Workplace' by Kashif Ali
'A Practical Guide to the Law of Medical Treatment Decisions' by Ben Troke
'Fundamental Dishonesty and QOCS in Personal Injury Proceedings: Law and Practice' by Jake Rowley
'A Practical Guide to the Law in Relation to School Exclusions' by Charlotte Hadfield & Alice de Coverley
'A Practical Guide to Divorce for the Silver Separators' by Karin Walker
'The Right to be Forgotten – The Law and Practical Issues' by Melissa Stock
'A Practical Guide to Planning Law and Rights of Way in National Parks, the Broads and AONBs' by James Maurici QC, James Neill et al
'A Practical Guide to Election Law' by Tom Tabori
'A Practical Guide to the Law in Relation to Surrogacy' by Andrew Powell
'A Practical Guide to Claims Arising from Fatal Accidents – Second Edition' by James Patience
'A Practical Guide to Asbestos Claims' by Jonathan Owen & Gareth McAloon
'A Practical Guide to Stamp Duty Land Tax in England and Northern Ireland' by Suzanne O'Hara
'A Practical Guide to the Law of Farming Partnerships' by Philip Whitcomb
'A Practical Guide to the Law of Unlawful Eviction and Harassment – Second Edition' by Stephanie Lovegrove
'A Practical Guide to Costs in Personal Injury Claims – Second Edition' by Matthew Hoe
'A Practical Guide to the General Data Protection Regulation (GDPR) – Second Edition' by Keith Markham
'A Practical Guide to Working with Litigants in Person and McKenzie Friends in Family Cases' by Stuart Barlow
'Protecting Unregistered Brands: A Practical Guide to the Law of Passing Off' by Lorna Brazell
'A Practical Guide to Secondary Liability and Joint Enterprise Post-Jogee' by Joanne Cecil & James Mehigan

'A Practical Guide to the Pre-Action RTA Claims Protocol for Personal Injury Lawyers' by Antonia Ford
'A Practical Guide to Neighbour Disputes and the Law' by Alexander Walsh
'A Practical Guide to Coercive Control for Legal Practitioners and Victims' by Rachel Horman
'A Practical Guide to the Law of Driverless Cars – Second Edition'
by Alex Glassbrook, Emma Northey & Scarlett Milligan
'A Practical Guide to TOLATA Claims' by Greg Williams
'A Practical Guide to Elderly Law – Second Edition' by Justin Patten
'A Practical Guide to Responding to Housing Disrepair and Unfitness Claims' by Iain Wightwick
'A Practical Guide to the Law of Bullying and Harassment in the Workplace' by Philip Hyland
'How to Be a Freelance Solicitor: A Practical Guide to the SRA-Regulated Freelance Solicitor Model' by Paul Bennett
'A Practical Guide to Prison Injury Claims' by Malcolm Johnson
'A Practical Guide to Advising Clients at the Police Station' by Colin Stephen McKeown-Beaumont
'A Practical Guide to Antisocial Behaviour Injunctions – Second Edition' by Iain Wightwick
'Practical Mediation: A Guide for Mediators, Advocates, Advisers, Lawyers, and Students in Civil, Commercial, Business, Property, Workplace, and Employment Cases' by Jonathan Dingle with John Sephton
'The Mini-Pupillage Workbook' by David Boyle
'A Practical Guide to Crofting Law' by Brian Inkster
'A Practical Guide to the Law of Domain Names and Cybersquatting' by Andrew Clemson
'A Practical Guide to the Law of Gender Pay Gap Reporting' by Harini Iyengar
'NHS Whistleblowing and the Law' by Joseph England
'Employment Law and the Gig Economy' by Nigel Mackay & Annie Powell
'A Practical Guide to Noise Induced Hearing Loss (NIHL) Claims' by Andrew Mckie, Ian Skeate, Gareth McAloon
'An Introduction to Beauty Negligence Claims – A Practical Guide for the Personal Injury Practitioner' by Greg Almond
'Intercompany Agreements for Transfer Pricing Compliance' by Paul Sutton
'Zen and the Art of Mediation' by Martin Plowman
'A Practical Guide to Adoption for Family Lawyers' by Graham Pegg

'A Practical Guide to Industrial Disease Claims' by Andrew Mckie & Ian Skeate
'A Practical Guide to Conducting a Sheriff Court Proof' by Andrew Stevenson
'A Practical Guide to Vicarious Liability' by Mariel Irvine
'A Practical Guide to Applications for Landlord's Consent and Variation of Leases' by Mark Shelton
'A Practical Guide to Relief from Sanctions Post-Mitchell and Denton' by Peter Causton
'A Practical Guide to Equity Release for Advisors' by Paul Sams
'A Practical Guide to Financial Services Claims' by Chris Hegarty
'A Practical Guide to Financial Ombudsman Service Claims' by Adam Temple & Robert Scrivenor
'A Practical Guide to Running Housing Disrepair and Cavity Wall Claims – Second Edition' by Andrew Mckie & Ian Skeate
'A Practical Guide to Holiday Sickness Claims – Second Edition' by Andrew Mckie & Ian Skeate
'Arguments and Tactics for Personal Injury and Clinical Negligence Claims' by Dorian Williams
'A Practical Guide to Drone Law' by Rufus Ballaster, Andrew Firman, Eleanor Clot
'On Experts: CPR35 for Lawyers and Experts' by David Boyle
'An Introduction to Personal Injury Law' by David Boyle

These books and more are available to order online direct from the publisher at www.lawbriefpublishing.com, where you can also read free sample chapters. For any queries, call us on 0844 587 2383 or email us at mail@lawbriefpublishing.com.

Our books are all generally in stock at www.amazon.co.uk with free next day delivery for Prime members, and at good legal bookshops such as Wildy & Sons.

We are regularly launching new books in our series of practical day-to-day practitioners' guides. Visit our website and join our free newsletter to be kept informed and to receive special offers, free chapters, etc.

You can also follow us on Twitter at www.twitter.com/lawbriefpub.

www.ingramcontent.com/pod-product-compliance
Ingram Content Group UK Ltd.
Pitfield, Milton Keynes, MK11 3LW, UK
UKHW021239300926
15471UKWH00013B/770

9 781916 698581